Japanese Children Abroad

BILINGUAL EDUCATION AND BILINGUALISM

Series Editors
Professor Colin Baker, *University of Wales, Bangor, Wales, UK*
Professor Nancy H. Hornberger, *University of Pennsylvania, Philadelphia, USA*

Other Books in the Series
Becoming Bilingual: Language Acquisition in a Bilingual Community
    JEAN LYON
Bilingual Education and Social Change
    REBECCA FREEMAN
Building Bridges: Multilingual Resources for Children
    MULTILINGUAL RESOURCES FOR CHILDREN PROJECT
Child-Rearing in Ethnic Minorities
    J.S. DOSANJH and PAUL A.S. GHUMAN
Curriculum Related Assessment, Cummins and Bilingual Children
    TONY CLINE and NORAH FREDERICKSON (eds)
Foundations of Bilingual Education and Bilingualism
    COLIN BAKER
Language Minority Students in the Mainstream Classroom
    ANGELA L. CARRASQUILLO and VIVIAN RODRIGUEZ
Languages in America: A Pluralist View
    SUSAN J. DICKER
A Parents' and Teachers' Guide to Bilingualism
    COLIN BAKER
Policy and Practice in Bilingual Education
    O. GARCIA and C. BAKER (eds)
Multicultural Child Care
    P. VEDDER, E. BOUWER and T. PELS
Teaching and Learning in Multicultural Schools
    ELIZABETH COELHO
Teaching Science to Language Minority Students
    JUDITH W. ROSENTHAL
Working with Bilingual Children
    M.K. VERMA, K.P. CORRIGAN and S. FIRTH (eds)

Other Books of Interest
Beyond Bilingualism: Multilingualism and Multilingual Education
    JASONE CENOZ and FRED GENESEE (eds)
Encyclopedia of Bilingualism and Bilingual Education
    COLIN BAKER and SYLVIA PRYS JONES

Please contact us for the latest book information:
Multilingual Matters, Frankfurt Lodge, Clevedon Hall,
Victoria Road, Clevedon, BS21 7HH, England
http:/www.multilingual-matters.com

BILINGUAL EDUCATION AND BILINGUALISM 15
Series Editors: Colin Baker and Nancy Hornberger

Japanese Children Abroad
Cultural, Educational and Language Issues

Edited by
Asako Yamada-Yamamoto
and Brian Richards

MULTILINGUAL MATTERS LTD
Clevedon • Philadelphia • Toronto • Sydney • Johannesburg

Library of Congress Cataloging in Publication Data

Japanese Children Abroad: Cultural, Educational and Language Issues/Edited by
Asako Yamada-Yamamoto and Brian Richards
Bilingual Education and Bilingualism: 15
Includes bibliographical references
1. Japanese students–Education–Great Britain. 2. Education, Bilingual–Great Britain.
3. English language–Study and teaching–Great Britain. I. Yamada-Yamamoto, Asako.
II. Richards, Brian J. III. Series.
LC3185.G7 J36   1998
371.82995′6′0941–dc21   98 29055

British Library Cataloguing in Publication Data

A CIP catalogue record for this book is available from the British Library.

ISBN 1-85359-426-1 (hbk)
ISBN 1-85359-425-3 (pbk)

Multilingual Matters Ltd

UK: Frankfurt Lodge, Clevedon Hall, Victoria Road, Clevedon BS21 7HH.
USA: 325 Chestnut Street, Philadelphia, PA 19106, USA.
Canada: 5201 Dufferin Street, North York, Ontario M3H 5T8, Canada.
Australia: P.O. Box 586, Artamon, NSW, Australia.
South Africa: PO Box 1080, Northcliffe 2115, Johannesburg, South Africa.

Typeset by Archetype-IT (http://www.archetype-it.com)
Printed and bound in Great Britain by WBC Book Manufacturers Ltd.

Contents

'Leaving Japan'[1]

When I was first told that we were going, I could not believe my ears. We were going to England! In the boring days in Japan, this sounded so fascinating to me, but I did not realise that it was the turning point in my life.

From the point of view of the position I am in now, there was a disadvantage in coming here. I would have gradually lost the language of my own country — Japanese. But there was also an advantage in that I would have had the chance to learn English — a useful language to know. Of course, I was too young (I was 8) to notice that kind of thing.

At school, my friends asked me various questions, but most of them thought that I was lucky to have the chance to go to England. I had been thinking the same thing, until the morning of the day of the departure.

Although my memory is vague now, I can still remember two of my best friends frantically waving their hands, until we disappeared from their sight. On that moment, for a short while, a strange feeling of loneliness — that I will have no one to play with nor to talk with — rose up. I felt as though England was going to be a totally different world.

I felt just the same when I descended the stairs of the plane, which had just landed at Heathrow Airport. I could not understand anything written, any announcement and any words spoken . . . How many times did I wish, 'If only I could understand it'. For this reason, I refused to go to the shops and answer the telephone, etc. If any question was asked I answered in the only words I knew — Yes and No, even if it was not the answer the person wanted. During the lesson at school, I just sat there and did not understand anything the teacher said . . .

Note
1. From a note written by a 13-year-old Japanese boy reflecting on his move from Japan to England at the age of eight.

Foreword

DAVID WILKINS

Societies have probably always been linguistically more complex than most people realised, but it has become a particular feature of the late twentieth century that substantial numbers of people now work and bring up families in countries where their mother tongue is not the language that is most widely used in the host community. In some cases this is a consequence of permanent migration; in others, those involved expect to return either in the medium or the long term to their country and language of origin. Whatever the particular circumstances, there is a common set of issues that concern both those directly affected and those who are responsible for determining how the potential benefits of this bilingual and bicultural experience can be maximised and the potential problems minimised.

What are these issues? To begin with, it is generally thought to be beneficial to be able to communicate effectively in more than one language, but can it be straightforwardly assumed that children brought up in a bilingual context will acquire that ability with facility and with the exposure to a second language having no impact on their first? Then, command of language is crucial for the process of education, but what if the language that is the medium of education is perhaps not that of the home, or if it is that of the home, but not that of the wider community? Further, is the extensive exposure to two languages and two cultures an enriching experience or one that challenges in a disturbing way the individual's sense of social identity? How well will those who return to their country of origin be able to re-integrate themselves into that culture?

The papers in this volume relate to a specific group, the Japanese community in the United Kingdom, which has found itself asking just such questions; but though the discussion here is specific to that community, the issues raised are relevant to members of all such communities wherever in the world they may be and whichever the specific languages involved. The work reported in this book originates in the long-standing interest in the

Department of Linguistic Science at the University of Reading in first language acquisition, speech pathology and second language learning and teaching. Against this background a research group was formed several years ago which included the two editors and several of the contributors to this book with the aim of investigating the language learning problems encountered by the Japanese community in the UK. This volume presents some of the findings of this research. However, it is apparent that if a full appreciation is to be gained of the problems that face communities like the Japanese community, such a programme of study cannot be confined to the narrowly linguistic but must include an examination of the wider social and cultural issues involved. It is for this reason that the contributors to this volume include not only linguistic researchers but also those in both the host and the Japanese communities who have professional experience of or personal interest in dealing with the problems of Japanese children resident in the UK.

This volume will no doubt be read with particular interest by members of the Japanese community both in Britain and elsewhere. However, its concerns are of no less relevance to other language communities, whatever their exact status, which find themselves in a multilingual environment. Given that such communities are found world-wide, I am confident that interest in this volume will go far beyond members of the community that it studies and that it will be seen as making an important contribution to our understanding of bilingualism in individuals and in society. Above all, I commend it to all who have an academic and professional interest in multilingualism.

Introduction and Overview: For a Better Understanding of Japanese Children Overseas

ASAKO YAMADA-YAMAMOTO

Japanese Children Abroad

Japanese business has experienced a dramatic period of expansion during the past 30 years (ISEK, 1995; Yamamoto, 1991). An increasing number of Japanese companies started to look for productive business markets overseas during this period, and manufacturers, trading companies and banks have sent employees into different regions of the world as part of their overseas operations. In 1984 the number of Japanese nationals living abroad for more than three months was 228,914, including children. The corresponding figure for 1994 was 428,342 (see Figure 1). In 1984 the number of school-aged Japanese children abroad was about 36,000 and by 1997 it was a little over 50,000 (Figure 2). With the addition of children who

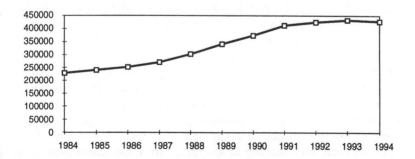

Figure 1 Numbers of Japanese residents overseas. Adapted from the Ministry of Education *Kaigai Shijo Kyoiku no Genjo* 1996.

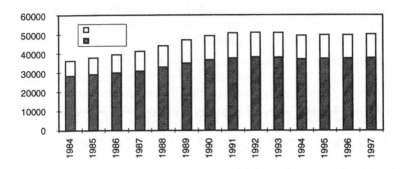

Figure 2 Numbers of Japanese school-aged children overseas. Adapted from the Ministry of Education *Kaigai Shijo Kyoiku no Genjo* 1996. Supplemented by statistics for 1996/97.

have not yet started school, there could have been as many as 100,000 Japanese children out of the country at any one time in recent years.

One characteristic of Japanese people living abroad is that they are in most cases only temporarily resident in their host countries. In 1994 the number of school-aged children who returned home after having spent several years abroad was approximately 13,000 (Japanese Ministry of Education, 1996). Until the late 1970s the general attitude towards Japan's young 'returnees' — those children who return from residence overseas — was not necessarily positive (ISEK, 1995). They were often perceived as 'problem kids' (Yashiro, 1995a) because they could not adjust to mainstream Japanese culture and its education system (Goodman, 1990). Teachers who received returnees in their classes were concerned about the academic progress of these pupils and found their ability to handle the standard Japanese curriculum to be behind that of the average Japanese child (ISEK, 1995). A particular concern was returnee children's lack of Japanese language ability. In addition, some children spoke English much better than their teachers, although they performed badly in their written English exams due to insufficient ability to translate into Japanese. Some children tried to enter into discussions with their teacher in front of the other children, something which was discouraged by teachers. Others experienced problems of identity and re-integration (Macdonald & Kowatari, 1995; Okada, 1993), sometimes leading to dropping out of the school system or, in extreme cases, even psychiatric problems. Pressure was put on returnee children to re-adapt to the Japanese culture and its educational and social systems as quickly as possible (Goodman, 1990), but this was not necessarily a solution to the problems of discrimination, self-esteem and confusion about cultural identity experienced by young people in particular (see chapters in Maher & Macdonald, 1995).

It was in the late 1970s that educators in Japan started to take an interest in young returnees. They observed the process by which these children readjusted to Japanese society, and saw that this readjustment sometimes caused confusion and conflict in both the returnees and those they came into contact with. On the positive side, educational researchers saw the study of such conflict as a way of clarifying the structure of Japanese society. Then in 1984, a National Council for Education Reform was set up, and one of the main themes was the 'internationalisation' of education (Goodman, 1990; Yashiro, 1995a; ISEK, 1995). In order to promote this national plan, the diverse background of returnees came to be regarded as an important resource (Goodman, 1990; Hirakata, 1990; Watanabe & Wada, 1991).

Such a shift in national consensus toward education has contributed to a change in people's perception of returnees, and currently there are many more opportunities than before for returnees to be positively accepted by both educational institutions and industry (Japanese Ministry of Education, 1996). It is nevertheless true that returnees still constitute 'a linguistic or minority grouping' (Yashiro, 1995b: 227) whose past experience is different from those who belong to mainstream Japanese society (Inoue, 1989; Ono, 1994).

In comparison with the increase in the number of studies on returnee children in Japan, there has been less information on Japanese children's experience of residence overseas (Okada, 1993; Hirakata, 1991; Minoura, 1984). This is probably because their cultural and linguistic problems become much more conspicuous once they return to Japan.

School-Aged Japanese Children Overseas

For Japanese nationals living abroad, one of the most important issues is how to adapt to the language and culture of the host country, at the same time as maintaining Japanese language and contact with Japanese society (Yashiro, 1991). Japanese language maintenance is particularly crucial for those who accompany children, since they know that they will return home in several years' time in most cases and that their children will have to readjust to Japanese society and the educational system eventually.

Strategies for addressing these problems vary, depending on each family's situation, the country they are posted to and the location of their employment inside the country. Some families concentrate on the issue of Japanese and send their children to Japanese schools; others send their

Table 1 Types of school attended by Japanese students overseas

	Japanese school only		Weekend school and host country school		Host country school only		Totals
North America	759	4%	12,277	67%	5,198	29%	18,234
Europe	3,633	32%	3,607	32%	4,152	36%	11,392
Asia	13,041	82%	267	2%	2,617	16%	15,925
South America	966	63%	78	5%	480	31%	1,524
Oceania	343	17%	393	20%	1,244	63%	1,980
Africa	173	33%	73	14%	278	53%	524
Middle East	291	58%	70	14%	140	28%	501
Total							50,080

Information supplied by the Japanese Ministry of Education, 1997

children to local schools or to International/American schools during the weekdays and to the Japanese Saturday School ('*hoshujugyoko*') at the weekend; still others send them only to the local or International/American schools. It should be noted that parents do not necessarily have such choice. In many cases they simply have to accept whatever is available to them.

For compulsory education (i.e. between the ages of 6 and 15 in Japan), the first choice of Japanese families in most cases seems to be the Japanese school (ISEK, 1995). Yet, since English is an international language, and a good command of English is necessary in the Japanese business world, many parents send their children to local schools in English-speaking areas or to the International/American schools. In the United States, which is not only an English-speaking country but also has a great influence on Japan in many respects, most Japanese children attend the local school (Table 1). Availability of Japanese schools also relates to this issue. There are in fact only two Japanese schools in the US: one in Chicago and the other in New York. Okada (1993) mentions two points regarding the tendency of Japanese children to attend local schools in the New York area: firstly, Japanese people's place of residence is spread widely; and secondly, despite a large number of Japanese children in that area, namely about 3500 pupils in 1993, there is only one Japanese school supported by the Ministry of Education in Japan.

In Asia, on the other hand, most families send their children to Japanese schools. This is partly due to unavailability of Japanese Saturday Schools in the areas where Japanese people live. In Europe, on the other hand, parents seem to have a wider choice than those in any other area in the world (Table 1). In Germany there are as many as five full-day Japanese schools and 10 weekend Japanese schools, while in the UK, there is one Japanese full-day school which the Ministry of Education in Japan supports, as well as eight Japanese Saturday Schools (see Chapter 2).

The UK Situation

Inward investment by Japanese commercial, financial and industrial organisations in the UK has resulted in a substantial influx into Britain of Japanese nationals who work in these enterprises, along with their families. In 1996 there were about 51,000 Japanese nationals in Britain (Embassy of Japan, 1996). In 1995, it was estimated that there were more than 10,000 Japanese children in the UK. There are two linguistic issues that concern the parents of these Japanese children. They are keen for the child to make as much progress in English as possible during their residence in Britain. But they are equally anxious that the temporary posting to Britain does not adversely affect the children's development or maintenance of their mother tongue which could result in educational and social disadvantage on the family's return to Japan. Our survey (see Chapter 1) shows that these concerns about language and the accompanying educational issues cause considerable anxiety for Japanese parents, and yet there is to date limited information or advice as to how such concerns should be addressed linguistically and educationally.

In such circumstances, this book tries to scrutinise the situation in which Japanese children are exposed linguistically, educationally and socially, by treating the UK situation as a case study of Japanese families whose employment makes them temporary resident in foreign countries. This volume compiles the expertise and experience of people who have close knowledge of the Japanese population in the UK, whose contributions in the chapters that follow range from research reports to personal testimony. The aims of this volume are twofold: first to clarify the difficulties that Japanese children encounter from the linguistic, educational and cultural perspective; and, second, by exploring the views of people who with different roles and responsibilities deal with Japanese children, to seek appropriate solutions to these problems. It is hoped that a compilation of such information will prove to be beneficial to those who are involved professionally not only with Japanese children, but children of any national or cultural background who may experience a period of temporary residence abroad.

This volume is divided into several topic areas: the general background of Japanese children in the UK; language learning and educational adaptation; observations by local school teachers and other education professionals; views of Japanese Saturday School teachers and parents;

learning and teaching a second language. Each topic area has several chapters. The following is a brief overview of these chapters.

Language learning and Japanese children in the UK

In Chapter 1, Asako Yamada-Yamamoto presents a statistical overview of Japanese children in the UK, with information on their geographical spread, age range, length of residence and the schools they attend. The overview includes findings from a Language Environment Survey, which was conducted in 1994 by the research team at the University of Reading. One of many thought-provoking findings in the light of concerns over Japanese language maintenance and development is that, on average, children attending local schools are exposed to English for approximately seven hours per day and to Japanese for two hours per day.

In Chapter 2, Kazue Aizawa explains the situation at Japanese Saturday Schools in the UK. She mentions that within a total of only 80 hours a year (40 Saturdays a year with two hours' teaching each Saturday) it is hard to follow the same national curriculum set for children in Japan. She also adds that having to be able to read and write 2000 Chinese characters during the nine years of compulsory education poses a real difficulty for both the pupils and for the teachers.

Next, Michael Garman reviews the normal development of English by native British children for the purpose of giving a basis for comparison with Japanese children's acquisition of English. He emphasises that by the time a normally developing English-speaking child starts primary school, s/he has already become an effective communicator through the use of English sounds, vocabulary and grammar. Such a picture contrasts sharply with that of a Japanese child who may join a British classroom with no English at all.

Carolyn Letts' chapter entitled 'A speech and language therapist's view' examines cases of English-speaking children with language problems. She points out that a particular difficulty lies in distinguishing children with a real impairment from those whose lack of communication has less worrying causes. This is important when considering the assessment of children from other language backgrounds, because those with poor performance in English might perform perfectly normally if assessed in the child's own language. Letts also stresses the need to take cultural factors into account when considering the linguistic behaviour of children who are learning English as a second language.

In Chapter 5, Brian Richards compares mother–child interaction styles in English-speaking cultures with Japan. While there are similarities in the way Japanese and American mothers speak to their children, differences also exist. American mothers use language more for its own sake; they are more information oriented, and they spend more time talking. Japanese mothers, on the other hand, are more functional, are attentive to the child's needs, are less talkative and are interested in maintaining emotional bonds. American mothers are also interested in eliciting detail and ask for a lot of description about a single event, while Japanese mothers are less concerned with detail, and are satisfied as long as the children's contributions are cohesive. Richards also mentions the notion of 'empathy' stressed in the Japanese child rearing process. In Japanese this is 'omoiyari': the feeling of trying to understand how others feel and what others need, by observing others and putting oneself into the other's position.

Educational adaptation and the acquisition of English by Japanese children

In the first contribution to Part 2, Joanna McPake discusses 'dissonances' experienced by Japanese children in British classrooms, drawing on the research she conducted with her colleague Janet Powney (Chapter 6). She focuses on four areas of dissonance which were identified in this research and relates them to the differences between British and Japanese educational philosophies, educational assumptions and expectations which are held by teachers, parents and pupils in the respective countries. One of these dissonances lies in 'understanding the role of talk and silence in the classroom'. British teachers in general have a belief that children learn through talking. In the Japanese educational philosophy, on the other hand, children learn through listening to the teacher. Such a discrepancy can cause difficulty on the side of both the Japanese children and their British teachers.

Asako Yamada-Yamamoto then reports findings from her research into the acquisition and development of English by Japanese children in the UK (Chapter 7). Through a detailed longitudinal investigation of four young Japanese children acquiring English in a naturalistic situation, the study highlights differences, as well as similarities, in the way these Japanese children develop English in contrast to English-speaking children at similar developmental stages. She suggests an influence from Japanese word order, which is distinctively different from that of English (cf. Chapter 3 by Garman), in order to account for a much slower and a different route taken by these Japanese children in acquiring particular grammatical structures in English.

Observations by school teachers and other education professionals

Part 3 contains six chapters by professionals dealing with Japanese children of various ages at British educational institutions. These practitioners express their views and present their strategies for trying to help solve the language and adjustment problems faced by Japanese children. The role of these professionals can be seen to vary according to the number of Japanese children present at their schools, the ages of the Japanese children they deal with, and the locations where they work.

Margaret Pond, headteacher of an independent girls' school in North London, presents her observations on Japanese pupils based on the school's long history of accepting a large number of Japanese children aged between 5 and 18 (Chapter 8). She also describes various strategies and schemes which the school has adopted in order to meet the needs of these children. One such strategy, the use of 'The Cottage' is introduced. This is a place where overseas pupils, including Japanese, learn English. It is also a refuge from ordinary English-speaking life, because this is the only place the Japanese children can use their own language.

Ann Griffin, headteacher of a county primary school in Reading, demonstrates, with her colleague, Sue Allaway, how they assess language ability in bilingual children, who comprise about 10% of the total number of the pupils at her school. Samples of written work from six Japanese children show us how these children develop their English. One of their school's policies – assessing children's language ability through their mother tongue – is noteworthy, and is consistent with Letts' recommendations in Chapter 4 in relation to language impairment.

In her outline of general academic progress of Japanese children in her school, Julie Bunker, head of the pre-prep department of an independent boys' school in Reading, explains how the school teaches and gives assistance to those who come to the school with little or no ability in English (Chapter 10). She also points out that not only teachers but also the English-speaking boys are very helpful to these children. She adds that if the child starts school fairly late (e.g. six years old) he should be given some help in English on a regular basis. It is also important that the children should not forget English too much during school holidays.

Sarah Mitchell lists some of the difficulties encountered by Japanese children and their parents from the point of view of those who give support in schools with bilingual students (Chapter 11). Among these is the isolation felt by Japanese mothers. The fathers tend to work long hours, and it is left to the mothers to be responsible for the education of their children. It is the mother who is expected to come to school to talk with the teachers, and this may be a difficult task for her, partly because she may not be confident in her English. However, we believe that another factor is that coming to school on an individual basis is simply not what mothers are used to in Japan where the parents talk to the teacher as a group. This relates to another important issue that Mitchell raises: 'the lack of knowledge about the two education systems on the part of both the Japanese parents and the British schools'.

Mo Pickering points out four areas the support teachers need to focus on when dealing with Japanese children in the school setting: 'access to the curriculum'; 'in-class support'; 'support for the mainstream staff'; and 'the peer group setting for the child'. Among these the last two relate to the way in which teachers perceive Japanese children in their classes. Pickering says that teachers must be careful about the way they respond to another culture, since misunderstanding or unfamiliarity with certain cultural behaviour patterns, food, or artworks can bring about negative reactions to those cultures from other children.

Michelle Turner (Chapter 13) has acted as one of the interlocutors for our research project since it started (see Chapter 7). Her observations on the linguistic behaviour of the Japanese pre-school children include a fairly late development of verbs (see also Chapter 7) and the existence of a quiet, whispering stage experienced by most children. In this connection, it should be mentioned that all of these children were seen to talk volubly and out loud in Japanese in their home environment, reminding us of the point made by Pickering in Chapter 12 that 'a Japanese pupil, like any other person, will be different in different settings'.

Views of Japanese Saturday School teachers and parents

The four chapters in Part 4 are written by those in a strong position to promote children's Japanese language development. Although the roles of these people are different, one thing they have in common is that they understand the pressures the children feel, and since they share the Japanese cultural background, they are able to interpret the children's behaviour, something which is not necessarily fully understood by local British school teachers and pupils. Our experience from the research project suggests that the points raised by the Japanese teachers are shared widely by other Japanese Saturday School teachers, and that the mother's account in Chapter 17 is representative of many other Japanese parents in Britain (see also Chapter 1).

Emiko Furuya-Wise details the situation at the Japanese Saturday School. She discusses major difficulties encountered by Japanese Saturday School teachers in the UK which include limitations in class hours (cf.

Chapter 2) and the diversity and complexity in children's language ability and background. Furuya-Wise also makes clear the roles and responsibilities of the Saturday School and the special context in which the children learn Japanese. She also suggests the need for support for Japanese children in the UK by the Japanese community in the UK and from the Japanese government.

As a teacher of Japanese in the secondary division of the Japanese Saturday School, Kazue Aizawa describes in Chapter 15 the extent to which her students have to keep up simultaneously with work from both their local school and the Japanese Saturday School. For the older students who have to start thinking about British public examinations (GCSEs and A Levels), the main problem is how to find time. Aizawa says that quite often on Friday night, the night before the day of the lesson, her students stay up until two or three o'clock in the morning. She also emphasises the importance of the pupils' own motivation and the parents' continuous encouragement of their children. One weakness observed even in the top students seems to lie in the quality of their vocabulary, or the lack of more formal or literary vocabulary, and it is quite reasonable to interpret this in the context of limited language (cf. Chapter 1).

As a former teacher at junior and senior high schools in Japan, Mariko Sasagawa-Garmory compares the educational environment of the two cultures. Her chapter starting with the sentence 'A good pupil in Japan may become a bad one in a British classroom' provides ample examples which may potentially lead to useful and practical advice for both Japanese parents and British teachers. She also stresses the necessity for close cooperation between British teachers and Japanese parents.

Yumiko Shibata is the wife of a Japanese businessman who has been in London for three years. Her documentation of one of her sons' initial experience at his local school tells us how important it is to try to establish mutual understanding between the parents and the school. Much of what she narrates here has been experienced in many other Japanese families. Even the karate display by her son which frightened his peers initially is similar to what the present author's youngest son showed at his infant school when he did not have enough English. What is important is that a solution to any problem seems to depend largely on the parents' wisdom and effort and the school's own approach.

Learning and teaching other languages

In the first three chapters in Part 5, teachers of Japanese present some of the problems which their English-speaking learners of Japanese encounter. The reason for the inclusion of these chapters is that that they provide a mirror picture to the situation in which Japanese children are learning English while developing their Japanese in a foreign environment. This section finishes with a more general account of the bilingual language-learning situation in the UK.

Helen Gilhooly (Chapter 18) points out that speaking Japanese at beginner's level may not be particularly difficult, but that a real difficulty lies in the teaching and learning of the Japanese writing system. Such a comment helps to understand how difficult the task is for Japanese children overseas to develop Japanese to a similar level to their peer group living in Japan. Gilhooly also points out that Japanese is a typologically 'different' language, which gives her students a particular interest in studying it. If Japanese is so different for English speakers, English must be also perceived as 'different' for Japanese-speaking children.

Lydia Morey (Chapter 19) has the opposite experience to that of the Japanese children in the UK. As a British national, she was brought up in Japan and educated in Japanese schools until the age of 15. As a 'returnee' to the UK, she describes the culture shock she experienced when she returned 'home', and how even now her instinctive thought patterns are often Japanese. Among several areas where her English-speaking students find difficulty in learning Japanese, she mentions their general lack of basic concepts of how languages operate, and the lack of any awareness that the structure of English is only one example of many possible ways in which languages are organised.

Kiyoko Ito (Chapter 20) also notes the difference between Japanese and English and emphasises the difficulties arising from written Japanese. Learning another language is 'just like exploring a new world', she says, adding, 'aspects that are not familiar in one's own language can seem rather odd'. By presenting comments made by her adult students, mainly diplomats, who have previously learned other, mostly European, foreign languages, Ito highlights the elements of challenge and enjoyment in the study of the Japanese language.

The theme of this book is 'Japanese children abroad' with special emphasis on those in the UK, and the focus has been on these children and looking at them from different perspectives. However, it is also necessary to consider the broader context in which bilingual children are located in British schools, and Viv Edwards' chapter (Chapter 21) serves this end. She says that according to one language survey conducted in the late 1980s, there were more than 170 different languages spoken in schools in London. In a historical overview of second language teaching and multilingual classrooms, she draws attention to a major change which occurred in the mid-1980s in the way British teachers responded to children joining their schools with little or no English: a change from teaching in withdrawal classes to mainstream classes. According to Edwards this organisational change can exploit the emphasis on the role of classroom talk in learning by promoting interaction with other pupils and providing appropriate linguistic models.

Concluding Remarks

In Chapter 21 Viv Edwards also mentions an enormous change in attitudes to linguistic diversity. Previously, language and cultural diversity were perceived as problems, while gradually bilingualism has come to be regarded as an asset for both the individual children and for the school community. Such a conceptual change can be considered as parallel to the situation of Japan's young returnees.

We must not be too optimistic, however, as Edwards warns us, since there are still teachers or educators who advise Japanese parents to speak only English at home and watch English TV, for example. We are approaching the end of the twentieth century. We, as adults, are responsible for educating the children who will in turn be responsible for making the twenty-first-century world a better place to live. It is predicted that the world's population will be much more mobile, and in such a mobile society we will have to face the reality of a world of multi-facets, with multi-cultures, multi-values and multi-languages. We hope that this volume will make a contribution in this respect: we also hope that it will stimulate further research into various issues pointed out in the papers collected here.

References

Goodman, R. (1990) _Kikokushijo_. Tokyo: Iwanami Shoten.
Hirakata, S. (1990) _Culture Gap: Kikokushijo Taiken Report_. Tokyo: Magazine House Publisher.
Inoue, H. (1989) _Kikokushijo no nihongo kyoiku_. Tokyo: Dojinsha.
International Students Education Centre of Kawaijuku (ISEK) (1995_) Japanese Education_. Tokyo: ISEK.
Japanese Ministry of Education, Science, Sports and Culture (1996) _Kaigai shijo kyoiku no genjo_. Tokyo: Japanese Government.
Macdonald, G. and Kowatari, A. (1995) A non-Japanese Japanese: On being a returnee. In J.C. Maher and G. Macdonald (eds) _Diversity in Japanese Culture and Language_ (pp. 249–69). London: Kegan Paul.
Maher, J.C. and Macdonald G. (eds) (1995) _Diversity in Japanese Culture and Language_. London: Kegan Paul.
Minoura, Y. (1984) _Kodonomo ibunka taiken_. Tokyo: Shisakusha.
Okada, M. (1993) _New York kyoikujijo_. Tokyo: Iwanami Shoten.
Ono, H. (1994) _Bairingaru no kagaku_. Tokyo: Kodansha.
Watanabe, J. and Wada, M. (1991) _Kikokusei no iru kyoshitsu_. Tokyo: NHK Books.
Yamamoto, M. (1991) _Bairingaru_. Tokyo: Taishukan.

Yashiro, K. (1991) Kikokusei no bairingarizumu. In J. Maher and K. Yashiro (eds) *Nihon no bairingarizum* (pp. 61–92). Tokyo: Kenkyusha.
Yashiro, K. (1995a) Japan's returnees. *Journal of Multilingual and Multicultural Development* 16, 139–64.
Yashiro, K. (1995b) The right to speak: Language maintenance in Japan. In J.C. Maher and G. Macdonald (eds) *Diversity in Japanese Culture and Language* (pp. 227–48). London: Kegan Paul.

Part 1: Language Learning and Japanese Children in the UK

Chapter 1

Statistical Overview of Japanese Children in the UK and Language Environment Survey

ASAKO YAMADA-YAMAMOTO

Statistical Overview of Japanese Children in the UK

The number of Japanese people in the UK and their geographical and occupational spread

Currently there are nearly 51,000 Japanese people in the United Kingdom (figures for 1996 from the Japanese Embassy, London). In London itself there are more than 20,000 and nearly two-thirds of the total number of Japanese people in the UK live either in, or on the outskirts, of London (see Table 1.1).

The statistics in Table 1.2 show the breakdown of the total number of Japanese people according to occupation. We can see that 8000 people work in private companies, most of whom are Japanese. In many cases these people are in managerial positions. It is noteworthy that 14,000 are

Table 1.1 Japanese residents in the UK (most recent figures May 1995)

Region	Number of people
London	20,500
Outskirts of London	9,000
Bucks, Berks, Cambs, Oxon	5,000
Other England	9,000
Wales	1,000
Scotland	1,000
Northern Ireland, etc.	100
Total	45,600

Table 1.2 Japanese residents in the UK according to occupation, May 1995

	Employees	Spouses	Children
Private Company	8,000	5,000	7,000
Journalists	150	100	150
Self-employed	300	150	50
Academics	14,000	2,200	2,800
Government	250	150	200
Other	900	200	400
Total	23,600	7,800	10,600

academics, including students and researchers. The estimated total number of children (defined as those who are under 20 years of age, according to the Embassy's statistics) is about 10,600, of which about 70% are those accompanying their fathers who work for Japanese companies. In the next group come almost 30% of children who accompany their fathers (or mothers) in academia.

It has to be emphasised that those families with fathers working for Japanese companies cannot predict the exact time of their return to Japan. This is because Japanese companies do not normally disclose to their employees at the outset when they are to return home. Such a company policy, however, can become a problem for their children's education, because the parents cannot plan for their children's education during their stay in the UK.

The majority of those people who work for Japanese companies stay in the UK for three to five years and less than 10% stay over five years. In general, each family expects to go back to Japan within five years. The number of permanent residents is about 4000, which is relatively small. This corresponds to 8.7% of the total number of Japanese people in the UK. They are mainly those married to British people.

Japanese children in the UK: Age ranges and schools

Japanese residents tend to concentrate in particular areas. In London, such areas are St John's Wood, Finchley and Croydon. Because of this tendency, many Japanese children may be at the same local school and, as will be shown later, some schools have a large number of Japanese children.

Out of the estimated total number of Japanese children in the UK (10,600), the number who would still be of pre-school age in Japan (i.e. those younger than six years old) is estimated to be 5000. The number who would be of school age in Japan is 5600 (i.e. those who are six years or over). Note that children start school a year earlier in the UK.

Among the 5600 school-aged children, 800 attend the Japanese full-day school in London: a thousand attend other Japanese-medium schools, which include four boarding schools. A total of approximately 2200 children go to Japanese Saturday Schools, as well as local schools. The remaining 1600 children go to British schools or universities, or Japanese colleges.

As was mentioned above, Japanese children attending their local school tend to cluster in the same schools and Table 1.3 shows the top 20 local schools where a large number of Japanese children are accepted. One school has as many as a hundred, and at some the number of Japanese children comprises more than a quarter of the total number of pupils. If we add up the number of Japanese children in these top 20 schools it amounts to 760, which is about a third of the estimated figure for Japanese children who attend their local school and go to Japanese Saturday School as well.

The pie chart (Figure 1.1) shows the breakdown of Japanese children in the UK according to age ranges (based on information from our own language environment survey). It indicates that those aged up to three years form 21% of the total and those aged between four and six years form 25%: 46% of the total, therefore, are pre-school children as defined by the Japanese school system. The children between seven and nine years, corresponding to the lower grades in the Japanese system, make up 20% of the total, and those between 10 and 12 years, namely upper graders of the primary school, make up 15%. Children aged between 13 and 15 years old, corresponding to junior high school, form 12% of the total. If we total the above percentages, we obtain a figure of 93%, making it clear that most Japanese children in the UK either would not yet have started Japanese compulsory education or are still within the time span of Japanese compulsory education. This point is important considering the fact that most of these children will go back to Japan after a stay of three to five years, and will have to adjust to Japanese conventions including its educational system.

The Language-learning Environment Survey

Aims and method

With the above-mentioned background of Japanese children in the UK in mind, results of the language-learning environment survey will be introduced which was conducted between the end of 1993 and early 1994. The aim of the survey was to identify patterns in Japanese families

Table 1.3 Top 20 local schools where Japanese children attend (estimated May 1993)

	Schools	Location	Category	Type	Japanese children	Total number	Ratio (%)
1	American Community School	Cobham, Surrey	International	Co-ed	100	1200	8
2	American Community School	Hillingdon	International	Co-ed	80	500	16
3	The Mount School	Mill Hill, London	Independent	Girls	70	450	16
4	Mary Mount International School	Kingston-upon-Thames	International	Girls	59	200	30
5	Frith Manor Junior, Middle & Infant School	Woodside Park, London	State	Co-ed	50	350	14
6	Preston Park Primary School	Wembley, London	State	Co-ed	40	550	7
7	Bury Lawn School	Milton Keynes	Independent	Co-ed	30	500	6
8	Copthall School	Mill Hill, London	State	Girls	30	1050	3
9	Dollis Infants School	Mill Hill, London	State	Co-ed	30	300	10
10	Holy Cross Preparatory School	Kingston-upon-Thames	Independent	Girls	30	260	12
11	The American School in London	London	International	Co-ed	30	1000	3
12	Moss Hall Infant School	Finchley, London	State	Co-ed	27	250	11
13	International School of London	London	International	Co-ed	26	215	12
14	Moss Hall Junior School	Finchley, London	State	Co-ed	25	350	7
15	The American International School	Southbank, London	International	Co-ed	25	150	17

Table 1.3 Top 20 local schools where Japanese children attend (estimated May 1993) (*cont.*)

Schools	Location	Category	Type	Japanese children	Total number	Ratio (%)
16 Tasis England (American) International School	Thorpe, Surrey	International	Co-ed	25	600	4
17 Wembley Manor Infant School	Wembley, London	State	Co-ed	23	261	9
18 St. Mary's (C/E) School	Finchley, London	State	Co-ed	22	400	6
19 Garden Suburb Infant School	Golders Green, London	State	Co-ed	20	270	7
20 Garden Suburb Junior School	Golders Green, London	State	Co-ed	20	360	6

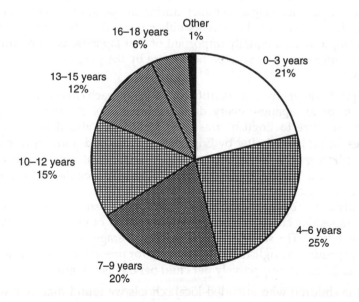

Figure 1.1 Ages of Japanese children in the UK based on the language environment survey, May 1994

regarding children's language learning environment and education. It was also hoped that it would be possible to relate the language performance of the children in our longitudinal study to factors such as age, time spent in the UK, schooling, motivation, effort and family language policy.

Approximately 100 randomly selected Japanese companies, government agencies, laboratories and schools in the UK cooperated in the questionnaire survey and agreed to release the names and addresses of Japanese employees. Questionnaires were sent to all the employees in those companies who had been sent from Japan and had children accompanying them. Of the 525 Japanese families contacted 320 returned responses, representing 61.3% of the total, which is pleasingly high for this kind of postal survey. The survey covered 591 children, and comprised 413 school-aged and 178 pre-school children. The total corresponds with 6.5% of the estimated total number of Japanese children in the UK. The questionnaire was written in Japanese, and had 42 questions. (See Fletcher & Yamada-Yamamoto, 1994 for further details; Richards & Yamada-Yamamoto, in press.)

Results of the survey

The major results of this survey are introduced briefly here. Regarding the Japanese parents' language policy during the period when they are in the UK, the majority of the parents either think that the Japanese and English languages are equally important or that Japanese is more important. The latter view seems to be held more by the parents of pre-school children.

The questionnaire tried to identify for how long each child was exposed to English or to Japanese every day. For pre-school children, the term 'regular exposure to English' was used to include 'attendance at local nurseries; being looked after by English-speaking child-minders or baby-sitters'; 'playing with English-speaking children'; 'watching English TV and video'; and 'having English tuition'. The term 'regular exposure to Japanese' was used to include 'attendance at Japanese-speaking nurseries; being looked after by Japanese child-minders or baby-sitters'; 'playing with Japanese-speaking children'; 'watching Japanese TV or video'; and 'having Japanese tuition'. The survey showed that the average number of hours of regular exposure to English and to Japanese for pre-school children was 3 hours and 2.6 hours respectively per child per day (see Figure 1.2).

For the children who attended local schools we found that they were regularly exposed to English for 6.9 hours per day, and to Japanese for 2 hours per day (Figure 1.3). 'Regular exposure to English' for this group was meant to include 'attendance at local school'; 'playing with English-speak-

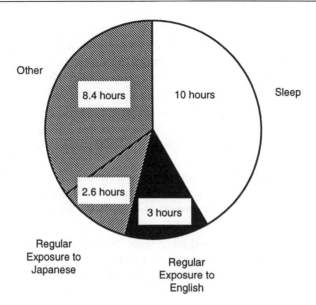

Figure 1.2 Japanese pre-school children's daily life in the UK

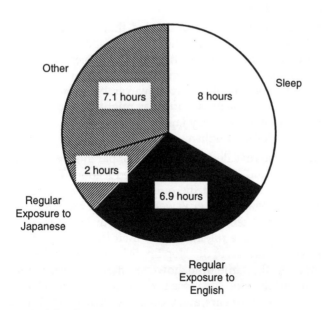

Figure 1.3 Daily life of Japanese children attending UK local schools

ing children'; 'activities using English'; 'watching English TV and video'; and 'having extra English tuition'. 'Regular exposure to Japanese' was meant to include time for 'attendance at Japanese Saturday School'; 'playing with Japanese children in Japanese'; 'activities using Japanese'; 'watching Japanese TV and video'; and 'having extra Japanese tuition'.

It has to be remembered that these statistics simply indicate the average time spent per day for all the children sampled in the two categories: pre-school children and school-aged children respectively. In fact, great variation exists in the amount of time of 'regular exposure' to each language. Moreover, nothing is known about how the remaining time, i.e. the average time of 8.4 hours for the pre-schoolers and 7.1 hours for the school-aged children, is spent. It is reasonable to assume considerable variation between children in this respect.

The questionnaire also asked parents about the language their children used at home with the parents and with their siblings. Approximately 83% of pre-schoolers speak to their parents only in Japanese, 14% with some English and 3% mainly in English. For school-aged children the picture is very similar: approximately 81% speak to their parents only in Japanese at home; 15% use some English and 3% use mainly English. As for the language spoken between the children at home, both pre-school and school-aged children tend to use English more with their brothers and sisters than with their parents.

Other findings of the survey showed that regarding the relationship between the length of stay and the language spoken at home, there is no significant correlation between these two variables, and there are many children who are using only Japanese at home even after 10 years' stay in the UK. There is some relationship, however, between the choice of school and the parents' language attitudes; as might be expected, parents who send their children to a full-day Japanese school tend to think that Japanese is more important than English.

The survey also revealed the existence of parents' worries and concerns regarding their children's language and education. This became evident from a section at the end of the questionnaire where respondents could write comments. Many concerns were expressed by parents who claimed that their children seemed to be delayed both in Japanese and English. Many parents were in a dilemma as to their language policy; they would have liked their children to develop English fully in order to adjust to their local schools. At the same time, however, they also wanted their children to maintain and develop Japanese because they would have to go back to Japan after three to five years, and would have to readjust. The parents were also in difficulty because they felt they lacked access to proper assessment

Table 1.4 Parents' concerns about their children's language and education

L2 (English)
Lack of evidence of L2 progress in speech even when there are indications of
  comprehension and non-verbal communication in L2 contexts.
L2 slow in comparison to previous L1 (Japanese).
Lack of contact with British families.
Parents' own poor models of L2 for their children.
Loss of English on return to Japan.
Individual differences.

School
Effect of lack of vocabulary on school work.
L2 literacy.
Lack of exposure to L2 at school.
Social factors at school: friends and bullying.
Lack of explicitness in teacher assessment.
Uncertainty about which language will be most useful for education of the
  children.
Settling into new school/ getting accustomed to educational system.
Concerns about (re-)adapting to Japanese system on return.
Lack of guidance from school about Japanese and English and educational issues.

L1 and L2, and Language mixing
Delay in both languages.
Desire to know what is 'normal' in each language.
Which language to speak to the child?

L1 (Japanese): Negative effects of L2 on L1
L1 loss.
Slow L1 development.
Slow development of literacy in L1.
Restricted contacts with other Japanese speakers.
Japanese for academic use.
Interference from English.

of their children's ability in both English and Japanese. They also lacked
proper advice and guidance on their children's development in both
languages.

Parents' worries and concerns are listed in Table 1.4. It is evident that
many items are directly related to the children's language development,
either in Japanese or in English. Their worries also include those related to
the interaction between the two languages, such as language mixing, and
the effects of the use of Japanese on the development of English (or vice
versa). Concerns were also related to children's school adjustment, both in
the UK and in Japan on their return.

References

Fletcher, P. and Yamada-Yamamoto, A. (1994) *The Acquisition of English by Japanese-speaking Children Living in Britain.* Final report to the Toyota Foundation (Grant No. 93-II–144).

Richards, B.J. and Yamada-Yamamoto, A. (in press) The linguistic experience of Japanese pre-school children and their families in the UK. *Journal of Multilingual and Multicultural Development.*

Chapter 2

The Japanese Saturday School

KAZUE AIZAWA

There are eight Japanese schools in the UK. Of these the largest is in London, with 1602 pupils. There is one in Cardiff with 94 pupils, one in Derby with 111 pupils, Hereford with 79, Manchester 85, Yorkshire Humberside 23, Edinburgh 63, and one in the north-east of England (Washington, Tyne and Wear) with 78. The distribution of these schools reflects the distribution of Japanese companies operating in this country. Although in Chapter 1 Asako Yamada-Yamamoto has stated that the average stay of Japanese families is from three to five years, most families have spent, or are likely to spend, more time in other foreign countries such as the United States, other European countries and the Middle East, so that the total time spent outside Japan can be much longer.

The Japanese School in London comprises three parts in accordance with the Japanese school system. First, there is the elementary, or primary, level for children aged 6 to 12. The number of pupils at this level is 1152, and they are divided into 48 classes, which means that the average class size is 24 pupils. This is considerably smaller than the average in Japan. At the Junior High level, for students from 13 to 15 years of age, the number is 258 in 12 classes with 21.5 per class. At the Senior High level, that is the post-compulsory level equivalent to the English sixth form, there are 93 students in four classes, averaging 23.25 each. These three parts — Elementary, Junior and Senior High — are the mainstream of the Japanese Saturday School. In addition, there are 'basic' classes. These are mostly for children of mixed (mainly Japanese and British) parentage who speak mainly English at home. There are 98 children in this category, in five classes.

There is a teaching staff of 82 in London, working on three sites — Acton, Camden and Croydon. The head and senior teachers are sent from Japan by the Ministry of Education, but all other teachers are recruited locally,

27

and they are mostly women — housewives and postgraduate students studying in the UK.

The Japanese School enjoys charitable status like other independent schools. It is funded, firstly, by tuition fees, but it also receives donations from Japanese companies operating in this country and also a subsidy from the Japanese Ministry of Education.

We follow, in the main, the Japanese national curriculum. In Japan the academic year begins in April and ends in March, and the same applies to the Saturday Schools in this country. An academic year is divided into three periods of unequal length. The spring term is from mid-April to mid-July; the autumn term, which is the longest, is from the end of August to mid-December; and the winter term, which is the shortest, is from early January to mid-March. There are no half terms and we normally teach on 40 Saturdays a year. The number of school hours is 2.5 per day, of which teaching is for 2 hours. Therefore, the amount of time we have for teaching Japanese is 80 hours a year. As might be expected, it is difficult to follow the national curriculum in the time available to us and this is one of the constant problems for teachers at the Saturday Schools.

The teaching is done with Japanese textbooks approved by the Ministry of Education, and they are all provided free by the Japanese government. The emphasis of the teaching tends to be on reading, comprehension and writing, with a certain amount of grammar taught in the higher grades. As a result, speaking tends to be relegated to second or third place, which is something I personally regret. I suppose it is due to the Japanese entrance examination system that we put emphasis on writing and reading, rather than speaking. Japanese and Chinese classics are introduced in Junior and Senior High levels. You might wonder why we teach Chinese classics at Japanese schools. This is because historically Chinese classics have played a similar role in Japanese culture as Greek and Latin have done in European culture. Therefore, a certain amount of Chinese classics like Confucius and Tang poetry are taught to the older students.

Contrary to popular belief, I do not think Japanese is a difficult language to learn. Just to learn to speak Japanese after a fashion, is not that difficult. The real difficulty lies, I think, in learning to write Japanese properly. Our ancestors many centuries ago incorporated Chinese characters into the Japanese writing system, and we still use many of them. People ask me how many Chinese characters there are, but no one knows. It is like asking how many words there are in English — there are thousands and thousands. But under the current educational system, children are expected to learn about 2000 of them in the course of nine years of compulsory education. The exact figure is 1945 characters which are in constant use, for example, in magazines and newspapers. About 1000 of those are taught at the Primary level; the rest at the Junior High level. This is a great burden on Japanese children, especially for those living abroad, as they are not normally exposed to written Japanese and have few opportunities for using Chinese characters. Having to learn 2000 characters, therefore, poses a real problem for them and also for their teachers.

Chapter 3

The Acquisition of English by British Children

MICHAEL GARMAN

Introduction

The purpose of this chapter is to make contact between aspects of child language acquisition in English children and the task that is faced by Japanese children who come to this country. Depending on their age on arrival, the Japanese children have reached various levels in learning Japanese, but they typically start from scratch on their arrival here as far as English language acquisition is concerned. I shall therefore concentrate mainly on the early achievements, in the pre-school period. Doing so is not to claim that older children acquire English as their second language in ways that are identical to first language acquisition: rather, we need to start from first language acquisition, by way of setting the scene. I shall try to capture the stage-wise acquisition of English in terms of a process of successive unfoldings of different layerings of structure.

The Pre-linguistic Stage: Sound and Meaning

Language is essentially about putting together the sounds of a particular language community with the ideas that are the business of human mental life. That is where children begin, and the first part of the story concerns the child's increasing control over these two areas — in the first year of life, we observe children achieving a broader repertoire of sounds, and greater stability of mental representations of objects, attributes and events in their world. It is difficult to talk sensibly about what sorts of ideas a child may start out with, and how those ideas develop during the first year of life. But it is not an easy matter, either, to document very precisely the sounds that the child is producing at this stage. Certainly there is brain development involved in each case, and other physical developments as well. For instance, sound development is crucially dependent on basic changes in the

30

shape and size of the infant's mouth in the first few months. But there are changes going on in the brain as well that affect the way sounds can be coordinated in sequence and which also affect the development of meanings. By the end of the first year of life, the child is ready to put sounds and ideas together in first words. These represent a major achievement, and herald the onset of the first linguistic stage.

The First Stage: First Words

It is important to note that the first words of a child may be a mixture of three different types. There are 'real' words, which are those recognisably modelled on those of the adult language, but they may be very few in number; in the first dozen or so words of a child's early vocabulary there may be only one or two real words in that sense. The rest may be child words, that is stable word-meaning complexes that appear to have no identifiable adult model. Where do such words come from? Perhaps they arise from the still limited sound structure abilities that the child has at this stage. A number of adult words may contain sound properties that are simply out of reach of the child's ability to adapt them to his or her own sound system. There may be half a dozen or so of such words for every real word. Finally, there may be 'empty words'; that is, stable word-forms that the child can reproduce in the same way on different occasions, but which have no specifiable meaning, much to the despair of the researchers who go in search of them.

It is this early vocabulary, then, that forms the basis of the beginning of 'language' — in the view of many parents, and of many researchers. According to this view, the achievements of the first year of life, in terms of sound and cognitive development, form the apprenticeship to this achievement. Of course, we have to make a distinction here between production (which we have been concentrating on so far) and comprehension: it seems certain that children already understand many more words than they produce before the end of the first year. This is an important feature of language acquisition, which appears in all areas and at all stages. However, we may, for the purpose of this review, restrict ourselves to the achievements of production, if only for the following reason: by and large, children produce what they already comprehend, so that the production measure is indicative of what is most truly complete about the child's knowledge of his or her language.

So we may say that, of all the distinct aspects of language structure and function, it is vocabulary that is put in place first. This may not be very surprising: what is astonishing, however, is the rate at which it develops. Initially the pace is gradual, with the child working towards 50 productive words (and four to five times as many in comprehension) over the six to nine months after the appearance of the first word. Thereafter, two things happen, each having a profound effect on the developing language system. One is the appearance of syntax — albeit in the form of the most embryonic two- and three-word utterances; the other is a spurt in the rate of vocabulary gain. These two events define the onset of the next stage.

But before we get on to this, let us first consider briefly what use the child is making of its earliest vocabulary. During this period a concept that is often used by researchers is that of 'holophrastic' utterances. This means that the child is not simply collecting vocabulary as a language acquisition device: the child is a human being who is using words to get things done. It has likes and dislikes; it wants things done again; it wants things not to be done again; it wants to request, command and affirm. It is using words with a purpose that is essentially like that which we associate with the use of whole phrases or whole sentences in the adult language. Hence the term '*holo-phrastic*' for the utterance-like function of this early vocabulary. This establishes a type of functional continuity between the one-word period and the next stage.

The Second Stage: The Emergence of Structured Utterances

This stage sees the next unfolding of language structure, which is the point where the child can combine words. These very first word combinations are very short — two to three words in length — and it is thought by a number of researchers that we cannot regard them as structured in any but a linear sense — a bit like beads on a string, and a short string at that. The child's grammar at this stage is often referred to as 'flat grammar', reflecting the fact that it generates only linear strings of words. It appears that these grammars may develop in either of two ways: by 'synthesis', that is the increasing juxtaposition of single-word utterances, a route that is marked by signs of effortful and non-fluent execution; or by 'analysis' whereby the child 'takes in' whole stretches of language, and reproduces them lock, stock and barrel, a route that is marked by fluent execution but initially not always context-appropriate occasions of use. We may say that the synthesis route requires the child to build up longer utterances from basic building blocks, while the analysis route demands an increasing segmentation and awareness of the elements of what has been superficially taken on board.

Regardless of style of acquisition, and primitive as it may be, this early child grammar provides the first evidence of the knowledge of positional classes of words. This provides the child for the first time with the ability to use the same words with systematically different meaning — e.g. *see me* versus *me see*. This is the basis for the development of sentence meaning alongside continued development of vocabulary meaning.

The order of words to some extent reflects the tendencies of the language of the child's community: English is a language with a dominant word-order pattern of subject-verb-object (SVO), while other languages exhibit other patterns, or it may be that it is difficult to determine whether there is a single dominant patter at all. Japanese is an example where researchers speak of a dominant SOV pattern. To this extent, a Japanese child who has established this pattern for Japanese is faced with a radically different dominant order in English.

These word order characteristics seem to be enough to encourage the other development at this stage which is the vocabulary spurt. It is as if once a child gets the sense that a noun-class exists, and is usable as a subject of a verb, or as an object of a verb, then further words in the noun class can be identified in the speech around the child, and acquired much more rapidly than before any syntax was available. It is as if the child is already alerted to the potential existence of such words, and is on the look out for more of the same. For example, if the child is familiar with *drinking orange juice* and is then introduced to *mango juice*, the possibly new word *mango* has a frame in the child's syntactic and vocabulary knowledge into which it can fit. Such integration of real-world knowledge with language-specific information is the basis for the phenomenon of the so-called 'fast-mapping' abilities that children exhibit for new words. It is, nevertheless, an astonishing observation that children acquire new words at the rate of 8–10 new words per week. Even more astonishing, a straight-line average, from one word at year 1 to, say 150,000 at 20 years, gives a figure of 20 new words per day. Clearly, there is much more to be said on this topic than we can attempt here. We shall merely indicate that vocabulary development is an early and phenomenally important area of language acquisition; and it is carried out in a way that is intimately connected with, and facilitated by, the acquisition of syntax.

It remains to be pointed out that the child appears to shift quite systematically from the more specific to the most general, in the acquisition of individual word meanings (at least for the most clearly documented cases of referring words). Typically the child will underextend the use of a new word — e.g. *shoe* will refer to particular shoes in the child's world, not all; then the use of the word will overextend, to cover other related items which are not included in the adult word's meaning — e.g. boots. Finally, the child's extension will approximate that of the adult. It may well be that the overextension phase is partially the result of a systematic perception of analogy, e.g. that *boots* are a type of the same 'footwear' class that *shoes* also belong to. This permits the child to talk about things that are not yet in its vocabulary, and still be understood. We may suppose that this type of strategic use of relatively restricted vocabulary implies the development of a further dimension of structure which marks the onset of the next stage of development — the vertical dimension, or the hierarchical nature of language structure, which is essential to adult-like abilities in both vocabulary and syntax.

The Third Stage: Hierarchical Reorganisation

This next stage is one of fundamental reorganisation. It is as if the system developed to this point is only a temporary bridge — basic, universal and quite possibly biologically determined — to the main business of language acquisition, which is to achieve control of the language-specific features of one's linguistic community. Before we get into this, however, we must not lose sight of the fact that during this period there are continuing developments, in both sound and meaning. After all, the process of the unfolding of language-specific core features of vocabulary and grammar places new demands on the sound system and presumably on the cognitive system also. It may be that language development, particularly from this point on, is a crucial factor in cognitive development, as well as vice-versa.

So there is a complex interplay here. The stage of reorganisation may take place round about two years to two and a half years in the normal monolingual child. At this point a child will have the ability not just to produce sequences of words (which to begin with may be not much longer than the two- to three-word utterances of the previous stage), but to structure these sequences in ways that reflect the child's increasing grammatical knowledge: e.g. that the verb and the object together constitute a predicate; and that the predicate has a subject and that they together make up a simple sentence or clause. That is to say, we have for the first time the development of a grouping of the beads on the string, resulting in vertical structure as well as left-to-right structure.

Other features that are characteristic of this stage are the development of language-particular systems of grammar, of which we may mention just three briefly. The pronoun system: pronouns like *it* have been used since the first stage but it is at the third stage that the child will appreciate that such forms belong to a system which is organised in terms of person (*I, you, it*), number (*I, we*), case (*I, me*), and gender (*he, she*).

To take the example of case, it is typical for the non-subject form to be used for the subject initially (e.g. *me do that*), rather than vice-versa. This may well reflect the wider distribution and frequency of the object form in the language. It is during this stage that such superficial tendencies will be tested and more adult-like marking of this type of contrast will start to develop.

Auxiliary verbs also start their development at this stage. These are verbs like *can* and *will* which permit the statement of actions to be modulated in terms such as 'ability', 'permission', 'certainty', 'futurity', and so on: not just *eat*, but *can eat*, and *will eat*. These forms are also crucial to the eventual development of mature forms of questions and negative-formation: not just *mummy push?* or *no(t) mummy push*, but *can I push?* and *I can't push*.

Finally, we shall mention affixes, smaller than, and attached to, words for example marking 'progression' of an activity in time (*eat+ing* versus *eat*), the past tense *walk+ed* (versus *walk*), the plural (*cat+s* versus *cat*) and so on. At two and a half to three years we see further grammatical developments coming in. Negation in English is marked on auxiliary verbs, so once these are acquired the child has the ability to say *can't* as well as *can, won't* as well as *will, mustn't* as well as *must*. They are also fundamental to the formation of questions, both of the *yes/no* type (involving the inversion of the subject and the auxiliary) such as *can I do that?* and of the type involving question words (so-called *wh*-words), such as *where can I put that?*

As well as these system developments, the child increasingly develops the ability at this stage to exploit the recursion of elements that are already in the grammar: *mummy and daddy, up and down, hot and cold, in or out, run or jump, naughty but nice* all demonstrate this recursion ability.

Conclusion

In conclusion, the child towards the end of the pre-school period has become an effective communicator through the use of English sounds, vocabulary and syntax. So much so, that we sometimes lose sight of how much there is still to learn. The frontier age of five years is increasingly seen these days as one where the child must make the transition from sentence-based grammatical developments to the skills required in constructing discourse, keeping track of more than one participant in a complex sequence of events, and knowing how to foreground certain aspects of the message appropriately for the needs of the listener. These developments take us well beyond our immediate brief, however, and we shall conclude our survey at this point, in the hope that we have conveyed something of the logic of English language acquisition in the earlier stages, and thereby shed some light on the task that confronts the Japanese child.

Chapter 4

A Speech and Language Therapist's View

CAROLYN LETTS

Clearly a speech and language therapist is really concerned with language impairment. By language impairment, I mean something that goes wrong with the development of the various linguistic systems that Michael Garman has outlined in the previous chapter. These may be delayed in development or they may be functioning poorly. A child who is a temporarily resident in another country and acquiring a second language is no more and no less at risk of this sort of problem than any other child. I want to make it clear that I would not normally expect us to come across language impaired Japanese children and I do not intend in this chapter to deal with specific cases of Japanese children with language impairment. Instead, I would like to discuss the difficulties therapists encounter when it comes to identifying children with language impairment and with assessing them and helping them afterwards. These problems to some extent apply both with monolingual English-speaking children and with children who have several languages; however, they tend to be vastly more complicated when a child is from a bilingual background, and especially when he or she is from a different cultural background as would be the case with Japanese children in the UK.

Children come to us through a referral system. Most of the common communication problems experienced by pre-school or early school-age children are identified by health visitors or teachers who have regular encounters with the children. Also, parents themselves may initiate referral because they are anxious. They may do this through their doctor, or health visitor or school. Professionals and parents become concerned about children for a number of different reasons, but probably the most common feature that worries them is the very basic one that the child just does not say very much. I have a rough list of some reasons why a child might not say very much, but there are probably more.

Firstly it may be that the child is excessively shy, and one of the difficulties we have is that people can tend to assume that there is nothing to worry about and that the child will talk more when he or she is more confident. This may be the case, but it may be that apparent shyness is masking a genuine communication problem. So we have to try to tease out those children with such problems. A second possibility is that the child does not speak the language. In an environment where English is the main language, a child who does not know much English obviously will not be able to talk very much. In addition, he or she may have different cultural expectations about the situation in which s/he is being observed. For example, in the school context monolingual English children may use language more, may interact more and may take more verbal initiative than children from other cultures where such behaviour may be considered inappropriate or discourteous. Such children may be accustomed to wait before speaking or to 'not speak unless spoken to', and this can lead to misunderstanding. To give an example from a different culture, it is known that some West African children avoid making eye contact with adults as a sign of respect. Eye contact is something that British adults seem to expect, and they may find interacting with West African children somewhat disconcerting. Professional British adults may also interpret lack of eye contact as the sign of serious emotional disorder or even autism. Plainly children who avoid eye contact out of respect are not autistic! It is important to be aware of these culturally driven features.

A third possibility is that the child may be self-conscious about speaking. This may be because he or she feels he has a problem with speaking and is aware of it; perhaps the child knows that s/he does not pronounce words in the same way as other children; perhaps s/he is self conscious about an accent that may be a regional variation within Britain or may result from speaking English as a second language; the child may have had the experience of trying to communicate through English and not been understood.

Where the difficulties arise from accent or dialect differences, or from poor knowledge of English as a second language, speech and language therapy is not an appropriate solution. The last two possibilities on the list do, however, involve the speech and language therapist. The child may have a learning disability, which is to say that s/he will have a difficulty learning a range of skills, including talking. Finally, and much more rarely, the child may have a specific language impairment. This is a highly specific difficulty in learning any language whether it is the first, second or third that the child encounters.

Our problem is to tease out the children with learning or language difficulties. We do not want a child who is shy, or who does not talk much in school because of cultural differences, to turn up in the speech and language clinic and to be prescribed a certain number of hours of inappropriate therapy. It may well be that advice and help can be given by more appropriate professionals, such as second language teachers; inappropriate referral to speech and language therapy may even delay the child getting the right sort of help. Speech and language therapists and some of the professionals who refer children do have a number of decision-making strategies to avoid inappropriate referrals, and some of these are helpful when we are seeing children from non-English linguistic and cultural backgrounds. For example, getting to know the child helps us with the problem of shyness. We may see a child in a number of different contexts over a period of time and at that point we are able to make better decisions than at first sight. Parental reports are taken very seriously and it is reassuring if the parent reports that a child speaks a lot more in other situations — in the home or with friends, for example. Parents are generally very accurate in making such judgements and where they are worried, there very often turns out to be a genuine problem. However, the cause of this worry may be somewhat different if a second language is involved. We know from our questionnaire survey (see Chapter 1) that many Japanese parents are worried not because they think their children may have some sort of disorder but because they are having to make difficult decisions about their children's language learning and education. Such worry is very valid but may obscure the therapist's decision-making process to some extent.

Observation of the child in different settings is a useful strategy where the child's first language is not English. We can at least see how much talking he or she is doing in different situations. A case history is also important as it may suggest whether there is something in the child's medical, social, family or developmental background that may indicate the presence of a disorder. Ultimately, though, the therapist needs to look closely at the child's understanding and production of language in order to decide whether there is a language impairment or not. This is the difficult part. For the monolingual English-speaking child, we have a vast battery of tests and procedures by means of which we can look at the child's comprehension and production of language, and decide whether it is approaching what we consider normal for his or her age group. When it comes to children for whom English is a second language we usually have very little information to go on. We need to assess in as many languages as are important in the child's life. This means finding someone who can speak the language, and even then there are many problems. We need to know normal patterns of development of the child's first language, which in this context would be normal patterns of development in Japanese. I believe there is a fair amount of knowledge within Japan about children's acquisition of Japanese. The period which Michael Garman refers to in Chapter 2 as reorganisation, where the child becomes sensitive to the more specific structures of the language, is important. This period is going to be very different for each different language, even if in the earlier stages it may be possible to generalise across languages.

In addition to knowing about normal patterns of acquisition of the first language, we need to know about normal patterns of second language acquisition under the exposure conditions that the child is experiencing. From the questionnaire survey we now have an idea of the most common patterns of exposure to English for Japanese children in the UK. However, we do not know what the significance of these exposure patterns is. How much English should a child of a particular age know, following exposure to English at nursery school for two hours a day for three months? What sort of grammatical structures will the child know about, and what sort of errors can he or she be expected to make? The research at Reading aims to discover the answers to some of these questions for Japanese children. It does seem to be the case that different patterns and rate of English acquisition are displayed by children from different linguistic and cultural backgrounds, and so it seems that there are few generalities that can be made across different ethnic groups. We need to look in detail at every single different language.

Finally, we need knowledge about how a child's linguistic behaviour may be influenced by cultural factors. There are likely to be features of the child's general behaviour, perhaps in a clinical situation, that may be very much influenced by culture, and which may have nothing to do with the existence or non-existence of a language disorder.

Chapter 5

Input, Interaction and Bilingual Language Development

BRIAN RICHARDS

In this chapter I shall discuss the way in which people talk to young children who are acquiring a language. In doing so I should like to pick up a point made by Dr Letts in Chapter 4 when she stressed that speech therapists require knowledge of how the child's linguistic behaviour may be influenced by cultural factors. My own research has been on British mothers interacting with young children mainly between the ages of two and three years. However, it has become increasingly clear as I have studied the research carried out in other linguistic and cultural environments that there are quite important differences in the way Japanese mothers interact with their children compared with British and American mothers.

It is well known that people talk to babies and young children very differently from the way they speak to other adults. This speech register is variously known as 'baby talk', 'motherese', 'caregiver talk' and 'child-directed speech'. It has been very well documented, particularly in middle-class societies in countries such as the UK and the USA since the late 1960s and early 1970s, although it is less well attested elsewhere. We know, for example, that in cultures like ours even before children start to talk, when they are still babes-in-arms, mothers treat them as conversational partners. They talk to them even before they can understand, treating the child's smiles, coos, cries, burps, and eye contact as turns in a conversation which is truly interactive. The language that they use to the child is distinct in many ways. It tends to consist of short utterances which are well formed and do not contain the grammatical errors and disfluencies which are common in speech to other adults. There are therefore few false starts and hesitations. Utterances are relatively simple in structure and contain little abstract language. The overall pitch is raised and the intonation is exaggerated, with a wide range between the highest and the lowest pitch, even within a single utterance. The tempo is much slower.

As children gradually become more proficient in language, their mothers have strategies to facilitate their contribution to conversation. Their style of interaction can be very supportive, involving the child in every way they can. Frequently they clarify their children's utterances. They reword them and upgrade them, filling in the gaps where children miss out words or inflections. At the same time, they use language to manage the child's attention and behaviour in ways which may help to provide a stable association between sounds and meanings. The language of parents and other adults is said to be 'fine tuned' — though maybe the use of the word 'fine' is a slight exaggeration. By that we mean that the incidence of these features changes as the children's language develops, and we talk about mothers' language being 'tuned' to the child's level of linguistic ability, especially their comprehension. As the child becomes able to contribute more to a conversation so the mothers expect more of them, and mothers' own language to their children becomes more complex (see chapters in Gallaway & Richards, 1994).

Many people believe that the speech modifications outlined above, and which occur not only in the language of mothers, but also of fathers, other adults and even older siblings, influence the child's development of language. In fact, evidence does exist that the frequency of some of these features, such as asking certain types of question and managing the joint focus of attention in early interactions with children, is related to their rate of language acquisition. It is also true to say that mothers vary in the extent to which they do these things and in the extent to which they provide a supportive and responsive style — something which has also been found to be a precursor of a faster rate of development. However, the extent to which these special modifications to the language addressed to children are *necessary* is much more controversial, because research has shown there to be a great deal of variation in the linguistic environment experienced by children in the different cultures which have been studied. Styles of interaction which middle-class Westerners may assume are facilitative or even necessary for their children's language development (like talking to them during the pre-linguistic stage) may be inappropriate in a different cultural milieu.

What is important to recognise is that children are not just developing a sound system, a vocabulary and a grammar, but are also acquiring cultural values through the use of language. In the conversations they experience, even at the very earliest stage, they are learning about their culture. Cultural values are deeply embedded in conversations between adults and children.

In gaining a deeper understanding of language, communication and culture, it is therefore informative to compare these early interactions across different cultures.

Of particular relevance to this volume is a body of research which brings out the contrast between interactions with children learning English and Japanese. Most of this work has focused on Japanese and American mothers, but I will start with a study that included a British dimension. An international project conducted by Anne Fernald and her colleagues looked at French, German, Italian, Japanese, British and American mothers and fathers interacting with their 10–14 month old children (Fernald *et al.*, 1989). It was found that these cultures did exhibit certain characteristics of the 'motherese' register, including the use of higher average pitch and exaggerated intonation, shorter utterances and longer pauses. This applied to all the cultures in which the research was conducted, including Japan, although these features tended to be most pronounced in the American mothers — even more so than in the British ones. It seemed as though this interaction style had three main functions. One was to engage and maintain the attention of the child; another was to convey emotional information and control levels of arousal. Finally, it served to clarify the language that the parents were using to an immature language user, to aid with the segmentation of the stream of speech heard by the child, and to highlight certain linguistic information.

Fernald's research found that the way in which Japanese parents spoke to their babies was very similar to the other cultures. However, some investigations have taken a more fine-grained look at conversations and analysed a wider range of features. Several of these have concentrated on mothers' language to babies as young as three months. For example, Morikawa and colleagues found that Japanese mothers did indeed treat babies of such a young age as conversational partners: they asked them a lot of questions; they talked about the child a great deal. But even at this early stage there were some differences in comparison with an American group. The Japanese approach was described as being more indirect, especially when controlling the child. Japanese mothers seemed to be more concerned with using the language to care for the child; they were very attentive to the child's needs and language was therefore very functional. American mothers on the other hand seemed to be using language more for its own sake; they engaged in a lot of talk containing a large amount of information, but which did not seem to be particularly relevant to the situation (Morikawa *et al.*, 1988).

Findings from a similar study, also of three-month-old children, are slightly different, but nevertheless consistent with those of Morikawa.

Sueko Toda and colleagues found that American mothers seemed to be more information oriented and asked more questions. By contrast, Japanese mothers were more interested in establishing and maintaining the emotional bond with the child. The latter used more onomatopoeic sounds like _'chikku takku'_ ('tick-tock'). They also used more nonsense words of a kind which would be unacceptable in the adult language (Toda _et al._, 1990). These findings mesh neatly with previous research carried out in the 1970s which suggested that Japanese parents were more tolerant than American mothers of their children's immature speech patterns, and that American mothers spent more time talking, while Japanese mothers did more singing, comforting, rocking and physical touching.

Perhaps what we are beginning to get a feel of here are some of the cultural values attached to talk as an activity. It would be impossible to give an exhaustive review of the research in this area, but a perusal of a range of key articles makes it apparent that certain key words and concepts occur regularly. For Japanese mothers the following descriptions are typical: 'more empathy with the child's needs', 'less talk', 'quicker to comfort the child', 'closer physical proximity'. Apparently, Japanese mothers were also _less_ demanding in terms of their children's politeness, an interesting contrast with American mothers who seemed to be very insistent on the child using polite forms of speech even to the mother. This only really seemed to matter in the Japanese families if they had a stranger in the house. In this case the Japanese child would be given formulae consisting of set phrases to be used in clearly defined situations. According to Clancy's (1986) study of two-year-olds, this concern with politeness to strangers and visitors extends at a later stage to ensuring that Japanese children develop appropriate turn-taking behaviour, respond when spoken to, and learn other speech norms. This is said to go hand in hand with what Clancy refers to as 'empathy training', which makes appeals to the feelings, desires and needs of others — learning to anticipate the needs of guests before a request becomes necessary, and understanding meanings and intentions which may not have been made explicit.

The notion of _'omoiyari'_ ('empathy') resurfaces in later research with older children. Minami and McCabe (1995) conducted a study of Japanese and American mothers' elicitation of narratives about recent events from their five-year-olds. One important finding was that the American mothers seemed to be much more interested in eliciting detail — a lot of description about a _single_ event, and a large quantity of talk in the story. They gave very explicit evaluations about the quality of what the child had said. Japanese mothers on the other hand provided less evaluation, but gave verbal acknowledgements in a way which reduced the length of the child's conversational turn. They were less concerned with detail but seemed more interested in eliciting a concise story which was a cohesive sequence of *several* experiences, a form of narrative which, according to the authors of the study, is particularly valued in Japanese culture. Another particularly interesting contrast in Minami and McCabe's findings was the fact that mothers in Japan discouraged the children from telling them things they already knew, while the American mothers actively encouraged this.

It is not my intention to present a stereotype here, and it is important to emphasise that maternal, or parental, behaviour varies extensively within, as well as between cultures. In addition, it is difficult to judge the validity and reliability of the research projects referred to, many of which had only a small sample of children — the largest study had 20 mothers in each national group. Nevertheless, studies carried out over a period of nearly 30 years, many of them conducted by Japanese researchers, do show a remarkable consistency in their findings. National differences in parent–child interactions reflect differences in adult–adult conversation, which in turn embody cultural assumptions about the relative value attached to various kinds of talk. The crucial question therefore for researchers, educationalists and clinicians is how we need to take these cultural values into account in our work as professionals dealing with both children and adults. If, for example, we as researchers wish to elicit language from young Japanese children who are learning English, then surely we have to understand the whole cultural context in which they have been born and raised, rather than just taking account of the fact that their first language is Japanese.

References

Clancy, P. (1986) The acquisition of communicative style in Japanese. In B.B. Schieffelin and E. Ochs (eds) *Language Socialization Across Cultures*. Cambridge: Cambridge University Press.

Fernald, A., Taeschner, T., Dunn, J., Papousek, M., De Boysson-Bardies, B. and Fukui, I. (1989) A crosslinguistic study of prosodic modifications in mothers' and fathers' speech to preverbal infants. *Journal of Child Language* 16, 477–501.

Gallaway, C. and Richards, B.J. (eds) (1994) *Input and Interaction in Language Acquisition*. Cambridge: Cambridge University Press.

Minami, M. and McCabe, A. (1995) Rice balls and bear hunts: Japanese and North American family narrative patterns. *Journal of Child Language* 22, 423–45.

Morikawa, H., Shand, N. and Kosawa, Y. (1988) Maternal speech to prelingual infants in Japan and the United States: Relationships among functions, forms and referents. *Journal of Child Language* 15, 237–56.

Toda, S., Fogel, A. and Kawai, M. (1990) Maternal speech to three-month-old infants in the United States and Japan. *Journal of Child Language* 17, 279–94.

Part 2: Educational Adaptation and the Acquisition of English by Japanese Children

Chapter 6

Dissonances Experienced by Japanese Children in British Classrooms

JOANNA McPAKE

Background to the Research

The research discussed in this paper was carried out between April 1994 and January 1995, investigating the educational experiences of Japanese pupils at school in the UK. The research, which was funded by the Economic and Social Research Council (ESRC), was carried out by Janet Powney and Joanna McPake of the Scottish Council for Research in Education.

The research took place in two thriving Japanese communities, one in Scotland and one in England. We looked specifically at Japanese children in the 11 to 13 age group, which was significant because they were between primary and secondary education. (Children go to secondary school a year later in Scotland than they do in England.)

We had three aims. The first, which is the one principally discussed in this paper was to look at areas of dissonance[1] in Japanese children's experiences of school in the UK. What we identified as a 'dissonant' experience is one in which children encounter contradictory notions of what school is: the roles which pupils should play, what makes a good pupil, and what pupils should do at school. We found that there were certain aspects of education, though not all, which contradicted Japanese children's cultural understanding of what school is, and what pupils are.

We also wanted to look at the extent to which teaching strategies in British schools could be said to be taking account of culturally diverse approaches to learning among pupils — not only Japanese pupils, but more widely. We wanted to ask: 'Are British teachers aware of these cultural differences, particularly in relation to educational expectations among

47

parents and among the children themselves when they are a little older? And how do they respond to them in their work in the classroom?'

Thirdly, we wanted to draw attention to aspects of our cultural construction of school that are often taken for granted. So we were not just looking at how the Japanese community saw school, but we thought that by seeing what the Japanese thought was odd about our school system we could question some of our assumptions. Our main paper on the research, entitled *'A Mirror to Ourselves?'*[1] looks at these issues in more detail.

Main Dissonances Identified by the Research

In this chapter, the focus is on our findings relating to dissonance. It is important not to think that everything about British school is odd or unexpected or difficult for Japanese children. Many aspects fitted in very well with their understanding of what school should be like. It is also important to be aware that Japanese children were doing very well at school on the whole. In Scotland, for example, where ability grouping is commonly used in primary schools, Japanese children were often in the top groups. In one or two cases, they were two or even three years ahead of their peers. It is not the case that Japanese pupils have enormous problems in British schools, but some aspects of British schools are difficult for them.

We identified four areas of dissonance:

- in understanding the role of talk and silence in the classroom;
- in the relative importance placed on knowledge and skills for learning;
- in expectations of academic achievement and educational aspirations;
- in notions of cultural identity.

In every case, we looked at both the Japanese and the British perspectives on these issues.

Understanding the Role of Talk and Silence in the Classroom

Looking firstly at the way in which British teachers understand the role of talk and silence in the classroom, very broadly it is the case that British teachers believe that one of the ways in which children learn is by talking to each other. British classrooms are set up so that children sit in 'tables', and they are either asked explicitly to discuss or collaborate on a task, or are implicitly expected to talk to each other about a task that they are doing individually. Even though they may be working on their own, there is an implicit assumption that they can talk about the work, ask each other 'What are you doing? What's the answer to this? Where did you find that piece of information?' Teachers do not mind — they even encourage their pupils to do this.

Japanese educational philosophy is that, by and large, children learn by listening to the teacher. The teacher talks, the children listen. They work on their own, in silence, and their learning is mediated entirely by the teacher. Certainly this may be changing now in Japanese schools, but it has been for a long time the prevalent model.

The effects of these dissonant experiences for the children are that they are often reluctant to speak in the classroom. There are two reasons for this. One is the very obvious reason which is that they may not feel entirely competent in English, although other papers in this volume have shown that, in fact, Japanese children have a high level of exposure to English, particularly if they have been living in the UK for some time. However, it is also the case that they may feel it is not quite right to speak out in the classroom. Some of these children have not been to school in Japan, but nevertheless they are getting messages from their parents, from the Japanese community at large, and from the Saturday School that one respects one's teacher and one of the ways in which one shows respect is not to talk in the classroom. For British teachers this is a very frustrating experience. Following their line of thinking, how can children learn if they do not talk? British teachers have a deep-seated belief that children learn through talking, through articulating their own ideas either to other children or the teacher. It does not matter that they have other evidence that the Japanese pupils are performing well: often they are doing very well in written tests.

One of the questions this work raises is how we adapt to different cultural expectations of education. Is the problem of silence all on the Japanese side, or do British teachers need to rethink their ideas about learning? When Japanese parents came to talk to teachers about their children's academic progress, they found the emphasis on talk somewhat baffling. When the teacher says things like, 'I think your child should talk more to the other children, should talk English at home, watch more British TV and less Japanese TV because that will help to develop their spoken English', Japanese parents think, 'What has that got to do with my child's education? This seems to be about their social life'.

Importance Placed on Knowledge and Skills for Learning

The second dissonance we identified was the importance placed on knowledge and skills for learning. Obviously, both British teachers and Japanese parents thought it was important that the children had both knowledge and skills for learning. However, the relative importance placed on these is slightly different. In British educational philosophy we have adopted what is known as the 'constructivist' approach, particularly when thinking about the education of children in the 11 to 13 age group. What teachers are primarily concerned about is developing skills for learning, and learning processes. They are not as interested in content *per se*. They focus on problem solving skills, skills for accessing information, but not dates, places, results of experiments. This may be changing with the National Curriculum in England and the parallel initiative in Scotland, '5–14'. However, historically, for the 11 to 13 age group, teachers have been principally interested in developing learning skills.

Japanese educational philosophy in this context is what is often called the 'information processing' approach. An important element in this approach is memorising facts. Again, this emphasis may be changing, but traditionally it has been a key feature of teaching and learning in Japanese schools. This creates particular problems for Japanese children who come to the UK and then return to Japan: however hard they work at their Japanese textbooks when they are in the UK, however proficient they have become in learning to read and write Japanese at the Saturday School, they cannot catch up with the amount of information their counterparts in Japan have memorised in the meantime. Interestingly, Japanese children do not seem to find it hard to move from the 'information processing' model to the 'constructivist' approach. Whether or not they had been at school in Japan before they came to the UK, Japanese pupils seemed to find it easy to adapt to British ways of teaching and learning. We are not sure why this is: it is an area which we need to explore further.

British teachers encourage parents to help their children develop these skills for learning, though Japanese parents may have found this difficult because, of course, their own background was in the 'information processing' model. However, what Japanese parents wanted to know when they talked to teachers about their children was about the content of the curriculum. They found it very difficult to get sufficient information. This may be changing, as teachers and parents become more familiar with the National Curriculum and '5–14'. At the time we were doing the research, these curricula were in place but still relatively new. Japanese parents found it frustrating that they were unable to find out what an 11-year-old should be studying over the course of the school year, and how their child was doing in relation to the curriculum. Had their child understood the topic? Would he or she have done so by the end of the year? Were there any problems? How could the parents help their child to overcome these? Japanese parents, as we know, expect and are willing to pay for extra tuition after school. British teachers, who do not expect parents to take this kind of action, are either unwilling to provide specific information about the curriculum and about children's progress in relation to it, or cannot see what use parents would make of this information.

Expectations of Academic Achievement, and Educational Aspirations

This third area of dissonance is connected to the previous area. In the past, British teachers have not, in our view, thought in great detail about educational achievement in relation to the 11 to 13 age group, precisely because the children are moving between primary and secondary school. We put considerable emphasis on supporting children as they move from one type of school to the other: we want them to feel happy, to feel at home, we want them to understand how things are going to work in secondary school. We want them to acquire the learning skills mentioned earlier, but achievement is not as important an issue. Perhaps it is because we realise there are many difficulties at this time in their lives and we feel it is not fair to stress achievement at a time when they may be experiencing emotional problems because of their age or because of the move to secondary school.

Another factor may be a certain educational elitism. Traditionally, few children in the UK have gone on to university compared with other countries. Things have changed markedly in recent years, but it is probably still the case that teachers, who grew up at a time when university was for a few people, retain the idea that only the most able will be successful. For the bulk of the children in their classes, it is not a realistic goal. This is very different from the position adopted by Japanese teachers, in a country where over 50% of the population go on to some form of higher education. In Japan, parents and teachers believe that pupils will do well if they work hard, and parents therefore want to do all they can to encourage their children to do so. Japanese parents in general have high expectations of their children's achievements throughout their school life, and this is likely to be particularly true of Japanese parents in the UK who, as we can see from other chapters in this volume, are likely to be academics and company managers. These are people who would undoubtedly expect their children to go to university in Japan and see no reason why British teachers would not have the same expectations of their children.

The effects of this dissonance are that Japanese children definitely work harder than their British peers. They do not necessarily achieve better results, but in many cases they do. What struck us when we were observing the children in this study was that only on one very brief occasion did we see a Japanese child not on task in the classroom. British children may be messing about, talking, reading comics, looking out of the window at times in the course of the school day, but the Japanese children were always working. Even if they have been educated entirely in the UK, they still seemed to have a powerful 'work ethic', and this tends to have positive academic effects. However, as one can imagine, it may have negative social effects in terms of the children's relationships with their British peers.

British teachers expect their classrooms to have a wide range of academic abilities within them, and also that individual pupils may display a wide range of academic abilities in different subject areas. To British teachers it is not at all surprising that a child may be excellent at maths and very poor at language work. It is not seen as a cause for concern because a child who is particularly able at maths would be able to go on to university to study maths even if his or her language skills are weak. It is a feature of our elitism: we do not expect all children to reach the class standard.

This is very different from the Japanese perspective, where all, or almost all children in the class are expected to meet the age-related standard set for their class. It becomes slightly harder as they get older. One teacher we spoke to suggested that about 95% of the pupils in a Japanese elementary school class should reach the class standard, whereas perhaps by the time they reach senior high school, this may have dropped to 80%. These figures are considerably higher than British teachers' expectations: some recent suggestions, in the context of national assessments in Scotland, are that the expectation for primary school pupils is that some 65–70% of the children in the class will reach the age-related standard. Japanese parents want evidence of their children's place in relation to the class standard. Usually, British teachers do not have any such evidence to give them.

Notions of Cultural Identity

The last area of dissonance is notions of cultural identity. This does not refer to what it means to be British or what it means to be Japanese, but what British people think cultural identity is and what Japanese people think it is. This is a more abstract concept. Schools in certain parts of the UK have, historically, considerable experience of working with children from a range of different linguistic and cultural backgrounds. In the 1960s, we expected children from different cultural backgrounds to become assimilated. More recently, we have developed a more liberal idea of integration: this means that we expect children from a wide range of cultural backgrounds to adopt British cultural perspectives and behaviour, although at the same time they can keep their own. The difference between assimilation and integration, to paraphrase the Conservative politician Norman Tebitt is that assimilation means children of Pakistani origin living in the UK must support England in cricket matches, whereas integration means that they can support both England and Pakistan. However, we do not understand what is gained and what is lost in the process of integration.

In contrast, in Japan, historically, there has been a strong belief in the uniqueness of Japanese identity. Many Japanese people believe that there are characteristics of the Japanese race which are not shared by any other racial group, and this belief is an important element of their cultural identity. When Japanese children go overseas, this can be seen as problematic. They may lose those unique elements of their make-up as a result of 'contamination' from contact with foreigners. This view of cultural identity is known as a 'subtractive' view whereas the British integrationist approach implies an 'additive' view. While not all Japanese parents would subscribe to this view, it is important to bear in mind that families who have come to the UK may not have chosen to do so and may not be particularly 'internationally minded' in their outlook. The integrationist approach adopted by British teachers can therefore be perceived as threatening.

The effect of this dissonance is that Japanese children can find themselves in a 'no man's land'. British teachers will always see Japanese children as, first and foremost, Japanese. This is to do with their appearance, apart from anything else. However long they have lived here, however fluently they speak English, however well integrated into the class, they will always look Japanese. Japanese parents, on the other hand, see their children as becoming more and more British over time, because they no longer exhibit all those unique cultural traits they would have maintained if they had stayed in Japan. Many parents talked to us of their sadness about their children moving away from 'Japaneseness'. This was not something they had expected, but something which became increasingly important the longer the families spent in the UK. Some long-stay families were beginning to recognise that their children would probably go to university in the UK rather than in Japan, because they did not have the necessary academic background, as we have seen, and were more 'British' than 'Japanese' in the way they approached their studies and thought about their futures. If they go to university in the UK, what is the likelihood that they will go on to work in the UK, perhaps live there permanently? They have to face the possibility that they may 'lose' their children.

Nevertheless, it is important to say also that Japanese parents see the benefits of internationalism. Their children are bilingual and they understand — in a way that Japanese people who have not lived in the West cannot — what Western perspectives are, how westerners think. This knowledge is potentially very valuable, particularly in jobs for which the ability to work cross-culturally is prized. As Japan and the UK are inevitably going to have closer economic and commercial links in the future, their prospects are good.

Note

1. Dissonances and other issues affecting the education of Japanese children at school in the UK are discussed in more detail in a paper entitled 'A mirror to ourselves? Educational experiences of Japanese children at school in the UK' given at the British Educational Research Association annual conference in Bath, 1995, by Joanna McPake and Janet Powney. Copies of this paper are available from the authors at the Scottish Council for Educational Research, 15 St John Street, Edinburgh EH8 8JR.

Chapter 7

The Development of English by Japanese Children Temporarily Resident in the UK

ASAKO YAMADA-YAMAMOTO

Introduction

In Chapter 3, Michael Garman showed how English-speaking (E-sp) children normally develop their own language. I will now discuss how Japanese children in our case studies have been developing English since their arrival in Britain. Vast individual differences exist in the way in which E-sp children learn English, especially in the rate of development. It can be imagined, therefore, that there would also be huge individual differences in the way Japanese children acquire English, since they are clearly different on factors such as age on arrival in Britain, amount of time of exposure to English, attendance at school, type of schooling, and motivation to learn the language. However, if there is any common tendency among these children's acquisition pattern which is different from E-sp children, it might be possible to ascribe such a difference to linguistic differences between English and Japanese, and/or to cultural differences which include differences in styles of interaction between people.

Background and Aims of the Research

The research described here originated in my earlier work, which was completed in 1992 (Yamada-Yamamoto, 1995a). It was a longitudinal, or long-term, case study of a three-year-old Japanese child learning English. Subsequently, a research grant was obtained from the Toyota and the Matsushita International Foundations in Japan for the extension of this case study to other children. For this purpose a team was formed in 1993 comprising Paul Fletcher, Brian Richards, Mike Garman, Carolyn Letts and myself. The study had the following aims:

(1) To compare Japanese children's English development with that of E-sp children.
(2) To identify any common tendencies, or patterns, in their development of English.
(3) To investigate interference from Japanese.
(4) To investigate educational implications regarding the development of English in Japanese children in the UK.

Research Method

To conduct this research, English utterances produced by five Japanese children were collected regularly every three or four weeks using audio as well as video recording. The Speech Clinic attached to the Department of Linguistic Science of the University of Reading, and the Japanese School in London were used for the data collection. Out of the five subject children, two have since returned to Japan. The data collection was made for 40 to 45 minutes per session through free conversation between the child and a trained E-sp interlocutor with linguistic knowledge. Every effort was made to keep each session as similar as possible. For this reason, similar toys were used and similar topics of conversation were selected, and the same interlocutor nearly always worked with the same child. The data were transcribed later, and then checked using the video recorder, and contextual information and non-verbal behaviour of the children were added.

The data collection started in May 1994 and finished early in 1998. Data analysis has thus been going on for over four years, and we would like to express our deep gratitude to the subject children and their families for their cooperation for such a long time.

In this chapter, data from four children will be introduced. These subjects were about three years old at the onset of data collection. They had lived in Britain for a relatively short period, and were regularly exposed to English through attendance at nursery or playgroup. They all spoke Japanese at home, and the parents of these children all put equal priority on learning English and Japanese. The three-year-olds were selected because it was considered that they would represent the most natural English language development: they had already acquired basic Japanese structures but had not yet been affected by the influence of formal instruction at school.

Findings

Individual development

Before discussing any general tendencies of these Japanese children, the development of the individual children, namely, Children A, B, C and D will be mentioned briefly. Figures 7.1–7.4 show the composition of utterances produced by each child in each session. The vertical axis indicates the raw frequency of utterances produced in one session, and the horizontal axis indicates the sessions over time. All the utterances were categorised into the following four groups: Japanese utterances; Minor and others; Major Single; and Major Multi-word.

'Minor and others' include responses such as 'yes' or 'no', interjections, and routines such as 'thank you' and 'I don't know'. Imitative utterances, unintelligible and problematic utterances were also included in this category. Other spontaneous utterances were called Major utterances, and divided into two categories: those made up of single words (Major Single), and those made up of two or more words (Major Multi-word).

Child A (Figure 7.1) started primarily with Japanese utterances which, as time passed, disappeared and were replaced by English. Although this child produced some Major Multi-word utterances in early sessions, they are all vehicle names consisting of two parts, which are incidentally phonetically the same in Japanese words. This state of affairs continued for several months. However, in Session 12, after the child had spent a month in Japan, he became quiet, with only a minimum production of Minor category utterances, Major Single-word utterances (mainly vehicle names and colour terms) and Major Multi-word utterances. Furthermore, in Session 14 there was no language production at all, not even of the Minor category. This stage was followed by the gradual introduction of fully productive Major Multi-word utterances. Intriguingly, the utterances

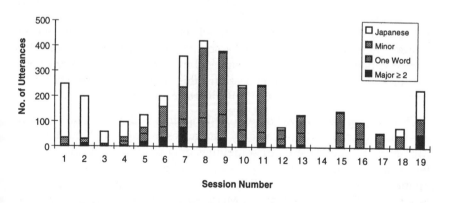

Figure 7.1 Total number of utterances per recording, Child A

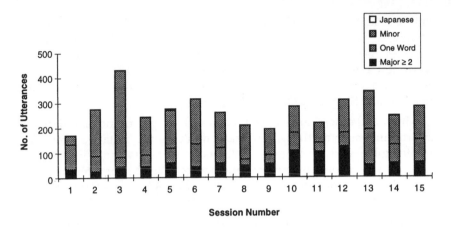

Figure 7.2 Total number of utterances per recording, Child B

produced from that point were mostly whispered. It is worth noting in the light of the increased production of all utterance types, and particularly the high proportion of Major Multi-word utterances, in Session 19 that this occurred three weeks after the child started at primary school.

Child B (Figure 7.2) used very little Japanese at any time, but in most early sessions this child's utterances consisted mainly of Minor category utterances such as 'yeah' and 'oh dear', and semi-formulaic utterances such as 'what(s) that' and 'here your are', 'look at that' or 'how about this?' These semi-formulaic utterances were categorised as Major category utterances even though they could have been categorised as routines (thus Minor utterances). However, it was considered more reasonable to restrict the number of 'routine utterances' to a smaller number consisting of what seemed to be truly unanalysed formulae: 'I'm sorry', 'oh dear', 'thank you', and 'I don't know'. In the later sessions, this child's utterances showed a higher level of productivity. Child B started school after Session 12.

Child C (Figure 7.3) was quiet for a long time with production of only one-word Major or Minor category utterances in English. Almost all the utterances were whispered or sometimes only mouthed. During the first two sessions, the mother was present, resulting in a high proportion of Japanese utterances. In Session 7 there was no verbal production at all, and very little in Session 8 — just one Major Single-word utterance consisting of 'fruit'. In Session 12, on the other hand, the child produced a lot of strange sounds, almost screams. These seemed to be used as a substitute for utterances, although other forms of verbal behaviour were also suppressed.

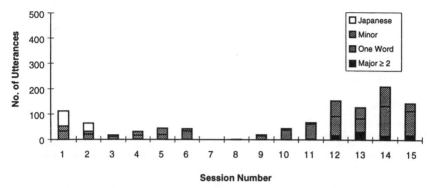

Figure 7.3 Total number of utterances per recording, Child C

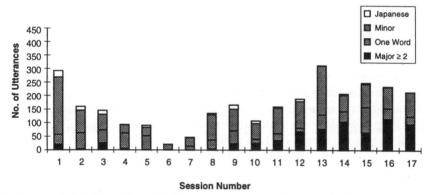

Figure 7.4 Total number of utterances per recording, Child D

This occurred after spending several weeks in Japan. After this period, the number of utterances increased. In later sessions, non-verbal communication including eye contact was observed much more frequently than before and the child became more facially expressive and looked much more relaxed. Child C started school after Session 14.

Child D (Figure 7.4) produced predominantly Minor and one-word Major category utterances in the initial period. Like Child C these early utterances were all whispered or even mouthed. The child became particularly quiet around Session 6. Then, in Session 7, utterances were either spoken aloud, whispered, or produced in a falsetto voice. Finally, in Session 8, utterances were voiced normally. Child D started school a few weeks before Session 15.

As a common characteristic observed in these children's development of English, we can note that all of them produced a large proportion of one-word Major and Minor utterances for a long period. Three out of four passed through a stage in which their production of English was either whispered and/or mouthed. It should be added, however, that all of these children spoke Japanese with me, normally, cheerfully and out loud, and their spoken Japanese development was considered normal for their age.

Utterance length

Utterance length is considered to be a convenient yardstick for the early development of English in E-sp children. For comparison purposes, utterance length of these Japanese children was analysed, and the mean length of utterance (MLU) of Major utterances was plotted against the length of residence every three months, as shown in Figure 7.5. The average for the MLUs of 'structured' utterances produced by the E-sp children studied by Wells (1985) is also shown in this graph. The results indicate that these Japanese children were at different stages of development. However, in general they show an upward, if sometimes erratic, trend. The children varied in their length of exposure to English, namely the time since arriving in Britain. The length of regular exposure to English (through nursery attendance) varied from child to child, as did the amount of exposure to English per week. Some children went back to Japan for a holiday once or twice during the data collection period.

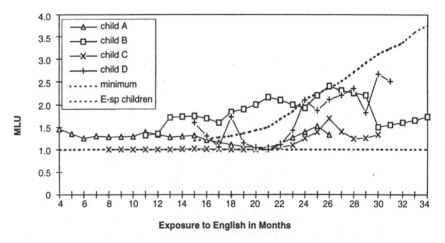

Figure 7.5 Development of MLU for English and Japanese children

To interpret these developments in MLU a number of points should be noted. For example, in Child A's utterances in the initial period, the frequent production of vehicle names consisting of two parts may have artificially boosted early MLUs. With regard to Child B, the frequent production of semi-formulaic Major category utterances mentioned previously (i.e. 'how about that?' and 'what's that?') may have inflated MLUs in the initial period. Child C did not start producing multi-word utterances until much later, and for this reason the MLU remained at 1.0 for many months.

From these circumstances, it can be surmised that the rate of MLU development of the Japanese children is rather slow in comparison with the general tendency of young E-sp children. Since the Japanese children were more advanced than the younger E-sp children in terms of cognitive and motor development, they might possibly have shown quicker development in combining words. In fact their development was slower. This may indicate that there is some fundamental learning difficulty in combining words, which comes from the difference in basic structure of the two languages involved.

Utterance patterns

There are several important findings regarding utterance patterns, or word combination patterns, produced by these Japanese children. Firstly, in the phrasal category of utterances, noun phrases were produced almost exclusively by these children at the earliest stage, and among the noun phrases, the combinations Adjective + Noun and Noun + Noun for possessive meaning were produced most frequently. Examples of the Adjective + Noun combination include 'green truck' and 'big house', and examples of the Noun + Noun (for the possessive meaning) include 'Michelle tractor' (for 'Michelle's tractor') and 'man hat' (for 'a man's hat'). It is noteworthy that the constituent orders to represent these grammatical relations are the same in English and Japanese.

Secondly, within the sentential category of utterances for declarative meanings, the Subject + Complement (SC) pattern were produced the earliest by children A, B and D. This can be seen in Figure 7.6.

Figure 7.6 also shows that the SC pattern was produced most frequently by children A and D throughout the period of data collection and was also relatively frequent for Child B. Separate detailed analysis of the SC constructions suggest that this pattern became productive first for all children. It should be noted that the constituent orders to represent the SC relation are the same in English and Japanese.

Thirdly, another utterance pattern produced relatively frequently by children B, C, and D was the Subject + Verb + X (or SVX), where X is usually

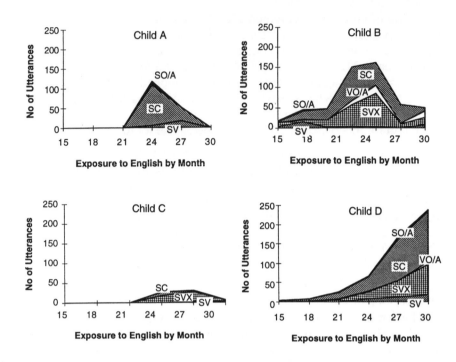

Figure 7.6 Utterance patterns for Japanese Children

the Object or the Adverbial of the sentence. Child C in particular produced a high proportion of utterances in the SVX pattern.

The characteristics observed so far in these Japanese children regarding utterance types is markedly different from that of E-sp children aged 15 to 30 months studied by Wells (1985). This can be seen from Figure 7.7. Because of differences in terminology and classification, the declarative utterances in Wells' study have been reclassified to correspond with the categories in the current study.

Figure 7.7 shows that the younger E-sp children produced steadily increasing numbers of SC, SV and SVX utterance types. From the beginning they also produced VO/A utterances such as 'see Jack' (Verb + Object) and 'go park' (Verb + Adverbial), as well as SO/A utterances, for example, 'Daddy car' (Subject + Object) meaning, 'Daddy is driving a car', 'Teddy there' (Subject + Adverbial). There was no tendency for any single category to predominate at any stage, but the E-sp children's VO/A utterances

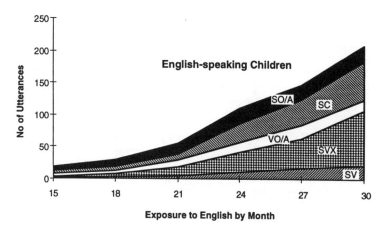

Figure 7.7 Utterance patterns in the Wells corpus

appear to have been productive from the earliest period of word combinations (Yamada-Yamamoto, 1995a).

By contrast, the Japanese children did not produce VO/A utterances in the initial stages of their development of English. Moreover, sentential patterns such as SVO which were produced frequently in the beginning by these children were not necessarily productive. They seem to have been produced in a fomulaic fashion. The case of Child B illustrates this point as is shown in Table 7.1.

Utterances of the SVO pattern were first recorded for Child B in the 13th month of exposure in the form of 'you did it' which was produced three times in the same session to mean, 'I did it'. In the 16th month, six instances of the SVO pattern using the verb 'think' were recorded such as 'I think[u] . man', 'I think[u] . that', and 'I think[u] . lunch'. There was always a slight pause between the verb 'think' and the following noun phrase. These utterances sounded as if they were based on the pattern 'I think + Y'. This pattern of SVO, however, disappeared quickly and such utterances have never been recorded since in the child's corpus. The pattern was, therefore, interpreted as being only partially productive.

In the 17th month, some instances of SVO were observed, which included 'you did it', and 'I c[∂]n do it', meaning 'I can't do it', but still no instances were recorded where the object was realised as a noun. While productive instances of the SC pattern increased continuously, the number of SVO instances also increased with different subject noun phrases and with different, but a limited number of verbs.

Table 7.1 Examples of Child B's SVO and VO utterances

Exposure length (Months)	SVO	VO
13–16	You did it (= 'I did it') I think[u]. man I think[u]. lunch	Open door (produced when the child took the lid off a toy kettle)
17–18	I c[ə]n do it (= 'I can't do it') You did it	Open the door (produced when the child pressed the lid of a box from where a toy animal came out)
21	You did it I got it I got it. flower	
24	I did it I fix it I got it I catch it (= 'I dropped it') I forgot. this I forgot. lunch	
26–27	I c[ə]n mend it You got the present I got the present I did the camera	Made it (= 'I made it') Did it (= 'I did it') Crash it (= 'I crashed it')
30	I get the Lego	Did it (= 'I did it')
33	I done it I broke it Mice don't get tails I making tea I watching Snowman	Open the door

In the 21st month, 'you did it', 'I did it', 'I got it' and 'you broke that' were recorded. And in the same session 'I got it . flower' was produced which could be interpreted as the precursor to the productive use of the SVO pattern. In the 24th month, the child produced 'I did it' (six times), 'I fix it' (three times), 'I got it' (twice), 'we got it' and 'I catch it'. In the same session, this child also produced the utterance 'I forgot. this' as well as 'I forgot . lunch'. The utterance 'I forgot. lunch' can be interpreted as the first real productive instance of the SVO pattern. In the 26th month, more productive instances were recorded, including 'you get the . present', and 'I got the . salad'. Interestingly, around this time, declarative utterances in the form of Verb + Object (or VO), where the subject of the sentence is missing, started to be observed. Examples include 'made it' (for 'I made it') and 'did it' (for 'I did it').

The development of Child B is closely paralleled by that of Child D (see Table 7.2). For this child, the SC pattern was already productive in the 15th month of exposure to English, but although SVO utterances were occasionally produced, mainly in the form of 'I want it' and 'I need it', this pattern did not become productive until after the 20th month of exposure to English. It was after the 23rd month that productive instances with a limited number of verbs such as 'want', 'like', 'got' and 'make' suddenly increased. It should also be mentioned that subject-less sentences started to be produced around the 29th month of exposure, which include 'carry the house' (for 'I am carrying the house') and 'need this' (for 'I need this').

Child C produced SVO instances both in a formulaic fashion and in a productive fashion with a limited number of verbs. In the 25th month of exposure, three instances of SVO were recorded, including 'I like . Bugs

Table 7.2 Examples of Child D's SVO and VO utterances

Exposure length (Months)	SVO	VO
15–18	I got it I like it I want it I need it	
21	I do it I find it I make it I like. rice I want. pink I make it flower Scott eat macaroni and cheese	
24–27	I do it I know it I like this one I draw. water I'm eat lolly	
30	I clean it I c[ə]n do it (= 'I can't do it') I clean the house I get the baddy I collecting the house I can get the snow I take the my house	Carry the house (= 'I am carrying the house') Need this Want this

Table 7.3 Child C's SVO and VO utterances

Exposure length (Months)	SVO	VO
25	I like Bugs. Bunny I like rabbit	none
26–28	I did it I need that I hold that You like red I got the book My brother seen it I got present I got sheep I got chips	none
30	I see my grandma and my grandfather (= 'I saw them') I read reading books	none

Bunny' and 'I like rabbit'. From the 26th to the 28th month, instances such as 'you like red', 'I got present', 'I got chips' and 'I got the book' were collected as well as 'my brother seen it' and 'I did it' (see Table 7.3).

Influence from Japanese

The discussion so far presented can be summarised as in Table 7.4. This shows that the pattern SC was acquired early. SV was also acquired in a relatively early period. Although SVX also appeared fairly early, its productivity emerged much later. The VO and VA patterns were also acquired later, while the combinations N + N for possessive meaning and Adj + N were acquired early.

Table 7.4 also shows the order of constituents of respective patterns in Japanese. It is well known that English and Japanese word orders are almost opposite to each other,[1] but patterns where English and Japanese show similarity include those of SC, SV, N + N and Adj + N. The table shows that when the structure of the particular grammatical constituents is different between the two languages, the acquisition of the target structure will be slower and later in the second language. On the other hand, when the particular grammatical constituent order is the same or similar in the two languages, the acquisition of the target structure will be quicker. It is probably the case that different word orders are difficult to perceive, difficult to produce and take more time to become productive; on the other

Table 7.4 Similarity and difference between English and Japanese

English structure	Japanese structure	Similar/Different	Acquisition
SC	SC	Similar	Earlier for L2
SV	SV	Similar	Earlier
SVX	SXV	Different	Later
VO	OV	Different	Later
VA	AV	Different	Later
N(possessive) + N	N(possessive) + N	Similar	Earlier
Adj + N	Adj + N	Similar	Earlier

hand, similar word order combinations should be easier to perceive, easier to produce, and take a shorter time to become productive. The data obtained for the Japanese children in their acquisition of English provide not only qualitative but also quantitative evidence to support this suggestion. It is particularly interesting that even the children as young as three years old have manifested the influence of Japanese in their acquisition of English in the fundamental word combination patterns.

Observations

It is noteworthy that the acquisition of the 'difficult' patterns such as the VO sequence seems to have been facilitated by formulaic learning. The role of formulaic learning has been generally accepted by many second-language researchers, and we would suggest that the experience of combining words in a different order in Japanese may have led these Japanese children, who are cognitively more advanced than young E-sp children, to look for longer sections, or patterns, in the English discourse around them, and to extract sections from it. The awareness of the sequence VO, for example, seems to have come from the extracted formulaic pattern SV + X (rather than S + VX) in which X functioned as O. The frequent use of the patterns such as 'I like + X' and 'I got + X', which were commonly produced by these children, may be evidence for this. The difference in the sequence of emergence of utterance types between those produced by a Japanese child in my case study, and monolingual E-sp children was discussed in Yamada-Yamamoto (1995b).

As a final comment, strategies to cope with the initial period should be mentioned. All the subject children managed the initial difficult period with the help of various strategies. These strategies include the following:

- use of Japanese words in English discourse;
- use of Minor category utterances;
- use of imitation of the interlocutor's utterances;
- use of formulaic utterances;
- trying to make the utterances sound more English (Yamada-Yamamoto, 1996).

These strategies seem to have helped the children in getting through the most difficult period of trying to keep communication going with their English-speaking interlocutors. Together with the fact that the two languages involved are typologically completely different from each other, this gives rise to acquisitional processes which seem more dynamic than those of most monolingual children.

Note

1. Smith (1978) proposed the 'mirror-image phenomenon' between English and Japanese constituent orders. Smith states that this phenomenon is commonly noted by persons familiar with both English and Japanese, and that 'a basic strategy for rough translations of descriptive prose from Japanese to English (or from English to Japanese) is first to identify the subject of the sentence, then to move to the end of each clause and work up' (Smith, 1978: 78).

    The phenomenon is typically illustrated by the example below, which is based on a Japanese language textbook (Hibbett & Itasaka, 1967: 118):

Tokyo eki   kara densha   de ichijikan kurai nishi e
Tokyo Station from tram   by one hour   about west towards
     15   14   13   12   11   10   9   8

itta tokoro ni Kamakura toiu machi ga   arimasu
go   place   at Kamakura called town (S-marker) exists
7   6   5   4   3   2   1

'*There is a town called Kamakura at a place (you can reach) going*
   1   2   3   4   5   6   7

towards the west about one hour by tram from Tokyo Station'
      8   9   10   11   12   13   14   15

References

Hibbett, H. and Itasaka, G. (1967) *Modern Japanese: A Basic Reader*. Cambridge, MA: Harvard University Press.

Smith, D.L. (1978) Mirror images in Japanese and English. *Language* 54, 78–122.

Wells, G. (1985) *Language Development in the Pre-school Years*. Cambridge: Cambridge University Press.

Yamada-Yamamoto, A. (1995a) *The Acquisition of English Syntax by a Japanese-speaking Child: From Left Branching to Right Branching*. Tokyo: Liber Press.

Yamada-Yamamoto, A. (1995b) The acquisition of English by a Japanese-speaking child: With special emphasis on lexical verb use. Paper presented at the Child Language Seminar. University of Bristol.

Yamada-Yamamoto, A. (1996) The acquisition of English by a Japanese-speaking child: The sibilant-sound attachment as an influence of Japanese. In M. Aldridge (ed.) *Child Language* (pp. 212–23). Clevedon: Multilingual Matters.

Part 3: Observations by School Teachers and Other Education Professionals

Chapter 8

Strategies Adopted in a School with a Large Number of Japanese Pupils

MARGARET POND

The Mount School is a private school with about 400 girls. We are situated in North London, very much in the diplomatic and businessman's belt. A great many Japanese families live in Finchley, Golders Green, Whetstone and Edgware — on the Northern Line because they can get to work easily. I think that is the major reason why Finchley and the surrounding areas are so popular with the Japanese families. We also now have some Japanese shops, but they are very expensive so everybody goes to Tesco's. If you wish to meet your Japanese parents you go to Tesco's on Saturday morning and they will all be there. So, to the great delight of the assembled throng they see the Japanese parents bowing politely to somebody who is rushing around with her shopping bag trying to get her shopping completed.

We have had Japanese pupils at the Mount School for some 20 years, and we realised very early on that even the most able Japanese pupil was unable to pass GCSE English Language with a grade C or above, and that their performance in English language was affecting their studies in other subjects. We have pupils from 5- to 18-years-old now, but we became aware of the problem when we thought primarily about the pupils coming up for public exams. We decided that we would address the problem by what we call 'special English lessons', and these take place when the English pupils have their regular English and modern language lessons. This means that every Japanese student in our school has one special English lesson every day. We think this is absolutely invaluable because there is only a short time interval between lessons and we can build on previous work all the time.

We are fortunate in that we have a little cottage in the grounds. It is called 'The Cottage' and that is where the lessons for the overseas pupils take place. It is just a tiny farm-worker's cottage that has been converted, and it has four little classrooms. It is not only a place where overseas pupils learn their English, but it is also a refuge, as sometimes overseas pupils are quite overwhelmed when they come to this country, not only the Japanese, but we also have Chinese, Russian and all kinds of nationalities. Students need somewhere that they can go to recover if it is just getting too much for them. So the cottage is open from 7.30 in the morning to 5.30 or so in the evening, and there is usually a teacher there. If they have problems they can go to 'The Cottage' and somebody will sort them out.

We have one full-time teacher who is entirely involved with teaching overseas pupils, and she has one assistant in the morning and another assistant who comes in for a couple of afternoons. We also have a student teacher who is a graduate and is going to do a Postgraduate Certificate of Education. It is invaluable to have someone young who finds it exciting to do things like this and does not mind keeping records. She will be the one to book the coach to take pupils to the theatre and organise their outings. It is exciting to do it for one year, but even though they all beg to stay for a second year, we send them away because in the second year it is no longer fun — it becomes a bore. In addition, if we find that teachers' timetables are light then we will put them in for a period with the overseas department, usually hearing reading or conducting conversation.

We started this about 20 years ago, and the number of Japanese pupils has steadily grown. We have between 35 and 50 Japanese pupils from 5 to 18 years, top heavy at the upper part of the school because when the Japanese schools finish their compulsory education at 15 or 16, they will come to us and say, 'Please teach us English and please arrange for us to study six GCSEs and three A Levels', and you have got two and a half years to do it. That is what we are sometimes faced with at what we call the top end of our market. Equally, we have the little girls who come in at five or six who are here with their parents. When we first started, we realised that the Japanese parents needed proof that pupils were studying well together. We therefore produced what we call the 'Mount School Overseas Department Examination Handbook'. In here we list all the possible exams in English which can be taken by our pupils, and there is a little blurb about how we go about doing it. When Japanese parents come to me to enrol their daughter, I give them one of these books and say this is the programme we will be following in English. We set each child a target for every half term or term. Sometimes it will be speaking, sometimes it will be writing and sometimes it will be listening. But we attempt to have some little exam or even a major one at the end of that time. This is not because we want them to do exams forever, but because their parents like them to do exams.

We have a record of what they have been up to while they have been in the school, and this is absolutely invaluable when our pupils go back to their own country because we are required to provide a document which they can take to their new school or use as a means of making application to a university. One of the jobs of our students is to keep this up-to-date. They update it every half term, and because it is on disk it can easily be printed out. We keep the information for every child in the overseas department. For example, one student's document includes: 'She took six GCSEs and three A Levels in just two years.' It also records her academic achievements and social activities. This particular pupil eventually went to an English university and she is now reading maths at Imperial College. She was here longer than most students, so she has rather more pages of activities. This system means that we do not forget anything because it is rather daunting if someone appears three days before the end of term and says, 'Didn't I tell you I need a reference?' If you have a few bits of straw you can make a few nice bricks.

We also became aware that the Japanese girls were desperate to learn something about English culture. Again, this was a problem we thought we ought to address, so we have what we call our 'Cultural Club'. Every term we arrange a visit to somewhere; for example, Windsor Castle or Brighton. We would arrange to visit the Brighton Pavilion or to go to Windsor Castle to see the Queen's doll's house. The visits are carefully prepared beforehand with a questionnaire that they follow through. So they really do learn to appreciate England through English eyes. We found that this was necessary because one Japanese pupil came to me one day and said, 'I went to Stonehenge and Brighton yesterday'. I asked, 'How can you go to Stonehenge and Brighton in one day?' She answered, 'Well I did.' So I said, 'What did you see?' She replied, 'I saw some tall pillars and I saw the sea.' That seemed to me to be a waste of an opportunity, and this is why we run these expeditions, usually on a Sunday to avoid Japanese Saturday School, but occasionally at other times. We also arrange theatre visits because, again, we think that helps with the English culture — it helps with listening to English people. Recently we went to see *An Ideal Husband* with the pupils aged over 15, which they enjoyed very much indeed. We tell them the story first so that it is not lost on them. Our younger pupils went to see *The Wind in the Willows* with the whole of our Junior School. They were prepared before they went so they knew what was going on. We also took the younger children to see *A Christmas Carol* at the Barbican, which was a wonderful feast of light and movement and drama, and they loved every minute of it. There was a little about English customs so we explained about Dickens and Victorian England.

Japanese students are used to having clubs and they feel very much left out without these. Although they can join the various clubs which are available at school, they do not feel comfortable doing activities like debating, so we arrange sports evenings, something they feel very comfortable with. They love playing tennis or rounders and in the winter we play games in the gym, which Japanese students very much enjoy taking part in. Also, because we want to involve the parents, we have presentations for their benefit. Students work on drama and music and we invite the parents to come, usually on a Sunday afternoon. Fathers are not always terribly happy because they would prefer to be playing golf, but we make it obvious that we are expecting them at the school. When the pupils put on a play, they will have painted the backcloth and prepared everything to do with it. They have already presented *The Pied Piper* and *Snow White and about Twenty-Three Dwarfs*. We usually adopt an English folk story for our requirements. As far as music is concerned, Japanese pupils are all very good musicians and they will play the piano and usually one of the senior girls will organise a recorder group for the younger ones. We have a very pleasant evening or afternoon.

We do try very hard to make the Japanese pupils integrate with the other pupils, and to do this lower down the school we try to arrange it so that there are no more than two Japanese girls in any one class, even though this is not always possible. Then they are forced to speak English, because otherwise it is Japanese chatter all the time. On the other hand, if you have a fellow countrywoman there, it means you have got somebody you can relate to if things are too awful. We say that they should attempt to speak English all the time except when they are having their lunch when they may speak Japanese, because we think they do need that little bit of a rest from relentless English. This seems to work very well. Of course, they do speak Japanese when they should not be speaking Japanese, and I usually say to them, 'What language is that?' Those that know me will turn to me and say, 'Oh, it's English of course'. Those that have only just come are mortified by the fact that they have been caught out. Again it works, because they have this feeling that, 'I have got to try — I must try to speak English.'

We do find that the parents worry desperately about what it going to happen when they go back to Japan, and usually in the first meeting I have with the parents I say to them, 'This sounds very discourteous but when are you going back?' When we know this we can arrange the older pupils' timetable to the best effect so that they can target the GCSE or the A Level examination. Then pupils will have this precious piece of paper with them on their return to Japan.

The school also has a Japanese mother who comes one day a week to teach A Level Japanese. However, she is also there to act as a help and comforter to us if we need it and she has translated part of our prospectus into Japanese. So when parents with little English contact us, they can take the prospectus away with them and read it at their leisure. We do also appreciate the long hours the Japanese fathers, especially, have at work, and I have frequently seen Japanese fathers at 7.00 or 7.30 in the morning so that they can get to work afterwards. This is greatly appreciated, but I think we do have to fit in with the lifestyle of these fathers because they work so tremendously hard. It helps with good relations.

We sometimes find that Japanese pupils are not terribly kind to each other. This worries us tremendously. A little girl who wants to have English friends may be ostracised by her Japanese friends who say, 'Oh, you are not being Japanese enough, you are becoming English'. It is worrying, because it is such a golden opportunity to learn English while they are here, and it does upset us when this happens. We try to get over this by saying, 'You are Mount School pupils who happen to be Japanese, or Hungarian or Israeli', or whatever they happen to be. It does help a little bit, but it is a problem that I think the Japanese community could think about and perhaps address. They do not need to lose their Japanese identity because of it, but there is just a little bad feeling sometimes.

One of the things we do is to give the Japanese pupils every opportunity to shine in front of the English pupils with things they can do well. We have just held an International Evening and the Japanese pupils dressed in their kimonos and there was a collective 'ah!' of approval as they all came in and everybody was very happy about this. They sang some songs and did a little presentation along with all the other nationalities. We also have Japanese pianists who perhaps play at school assembly — possibly a hymn or they play a little concert after assembly so that it can be seen by everyone that they excel at something, even if they cannot do something like history terribly well at this moment.

Although Japanese pupils have special English lessons, we do throw them in at the deep end with every other subject so that they have to have a go. This is where the cottage comes in because if they find they have to do something and they really find it very difficult we say, 'Gather the information, come to the cottage and we will help you write it down, but you have got to find the information'. Again that works very well.

In conclusion, I must say that we find our Japanese pupils a delight. Their mathematics is wonderful. We find that a child who can manage little else can be told to, 'Go and do a nice page of mathematics, dear, you'll feel much more cheerful then'. Now what English child would you say that to? It has raised the standard of mathematics in the school tremendously. We now have two-thirds of our pupils doing A Level mathematics — which is almost unheard of in an English girls' school — because they see the Japanese girls doing it. So we hope to receive Japanese pupils for a long time yet.

Chapter 9

Some Experiences of Educating Japanese Children in an English County Primary School

ANN GRIFFIN and SUE ALLAWAY

Introduction

Hillside School is a Local Education Authority primary school situated on a large private housing estate about half a mile away from Reading University and the Gyosei College. Families from all over the world move into this area for educational and commercial purposes and the school has 40, of 400 children, whose home language is not English. Children from every continent join the school without notice and the school has had to develop strategies to educate the children and especially give them a working knowledge of English as quickly as possible.

We have had the support of the County Multicultural Services to do this in recent times but in earlier years we had very little knowledge about the cultures the children were coming from and methods of educating them. Many of the concerns mentioned in other chapters were our experience too, the major ones being the short length of stay in Britain, lack of information about the standard of achievement by the child in their previous school abroad, the expectations of the home education system and our lack of expertise in teaching children with English as a second language.

As a result, we resorted to trying as many different approaches as possible. We found that, where the teacher and the English children were truly enthusiastic about communicating, the children's command of English flourished and much of the curriculum programme was available to the new arrivals from their very early days at the school.

We are going to demonstrate the children's development in English through some samples of written work from six Japanese children at Hillside. The school approach to writing is the Writer's Workshop

Method. That is, the children communicate their experiences to us using the letters that they have learned and the teachers discuss the work with them and transform the letters into acceptable English so that the child can build a repertoire of words for future use. Young children rely heavily on experiences at school and in their reading books. Older children have more freedom by using a dictionary to help convey the ideas they want to convey.

Case Studies

Child A

A boy in a Reception Class who is just five, demonstrates the importance of using experience that is in common with the rest of the class, as he draws his English house (see Sample 1). Children newly into school invariably choose shared subject material rather than material from their previous experience (and avoid speaking in Japanese). Notice that he is not very happy with his drawing and uses several lines to straighten it because he would like it to be square. Also, notice the numerous attempts to make his letters look just right. He has used seven of the letters from his own name and the teacher has written an acceptable sentence underneath using words he will have encountered in his reading book.

Sample 1 Child A, Reception Class, aged 5

It is important to note that we have come to realise the importance of the reading scheme books in the early weeks for children with little or no English. It is the link between the child, the parents, the teacher and the offered curriculum. The teacher reads the book and the child copies, gaining sounds and rhythm, if little else. The bilingual parent adds an explanation of text and pictures. Once the child has made the conceptual leap that English is just a communication code like the home language, it is only a matter of opportunity and persistence in learning before the child makes rapid progress.

Sample 2 Child A, Reception Class, aged 5

In Sample 2, Child A uses the initial letters that he has learned to indicate that he wants to write about his reading book characters. He writes 'B____', followed by 'a__ R____ a__'. In discussion with the teacher he supplies the extra letters and the word 'playing', needed for everyone to understand. This is within a month of starting school. He is reading every day at school, and at night his parents help him too. He is also learning phonics by means of a pictogram system called Letterland. He is making very good progress.

Child B

The work of this six-year-old boy shows the progress that a child can make in a year. He has had similar experience to Child A, the same teacher and the same programme of work. Sample 3 represents an important step, as previously when asked to write a story he repeated the same well-known story of *Goldilocks and the Three Bears*, many times. The rehearsal obviously has served him well, as he is able to write the story of *The Apple Tree* very fluently. There is no punctuation but the story flows in such a way that the reader can easily make sense of the writing. The teacher has added a few words to help continuity, something that the boy does not realise is required at this stage of his language development. The story has a well-defined beginning and end. It was shared with the class and recognised as a very good piece of work.

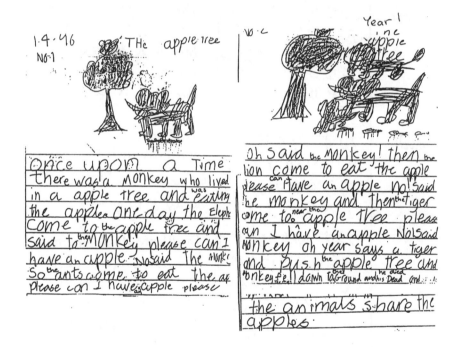

Sample 3 Child B, Year 1, aged 6

Child C

Child C had been in England and at school for only a week when Sample 4 was written. This boy had been to school for a year in Hokkaido, and on arrival at Hillside we followed the school policy of trying to find out all we could about his education in Japan and inviting his mother to spend time to work with her son in the classroom. She agreed to attend every English lesson. Child C was able to show how well he could write in Japanese, and

first draft
with mum helping
Japanese as first language

Thursday, 28th, March, 1996

YOH

How the mouse Fooled the Fox.

Introduction

しっぽ が くろと きいろ。
大きい。しっぽです。
からだが、ふわっとあ
たかい、からだ、森
の中のおはなしで
す。
きつねは。

The Fox has a big tail
with black and yellow.t
His body is soft and
warm.
This story is in the woo.

middle

ねずみを見つけ
て、おいかけた。も
ちろんねずみもてっ
しでにげます。

The Fox find the Mouse
and ran after him.
Of couse the Mouse ran
away very quickly.

End.

ねずみは、はしって
そこをみぎにまがる
といいものがあるよ。
といってにげました。

「あやしいけどま
あいいや、とおもい
ました。やっときつね
から、ねずみは
にげれました。

The Mouse told the Fox
"Turn the right next
corner, you can find
very nice things."

The Fox wonder it's not
trueth.
But it's OK.
I'll go he thought

At last the mouth

Sample 4 Child C, Year 3, aged 7

his mother's translation alongside the story gave him a useful range of English vocabulary in a context he understood. The reading scheme book helped with sentence structure and rapid progress was made.

In Sample 5, the same boy's self-assessment, which was written in the same way, helped to bridge the language gap and helped the children to understand that they had similar concerns.

Child's comments:

ぼくは、たいいくとかさんすうがすきです。たいいくのなわとびやさんすうのけいさんがとくいです。バイオリンをならっています。こんしゅうの金よう日からトンプソン先生にならいます。ぼくは、サッカーも大すきです。

こくごとえいごのべんきょうをがんばります。ぼくハムスターもかいたいです。バイオリンもがんばりま

I like P.E. and Math. I'm good at rope skipping in P.E. and calculation in Math. I have learned violin.. I will get violin lessons by Mrs. Thompson from this Fryday.
I like foot ball very much.
I think I need to improve at English and Japanese languages
I do my best for violin lessons, too.
I would like to keep a hamster as a pet.

Date 28. 3. 96.

Sample 5 Child C, Year 3, aged 7

How the mouse foomled the fox .

One day a fox was a greit champios
Of caching mouse. becose he won't to caiit.
Sox got his own big house and. next day
the fox went to go to forest to cach a
mouse he faund the mouse ne. grabetd. but he
misst. the children siait go on fox your good
at caching fox. Sox begen to be closs
n to claey mouse was raging children beg.
to be very closs and the fox begen
drid the mouse get got the pin. Subite on
foxsis heriy Taile and the fox Scream
help but mause did'nt help the fox
but the children did help mause said way
did you help. Sox ASede. childrem said
becose we like the fox children Said
bad fox and children said ayen his Very
he is very good fox
Said the All the children to us
to bi very closs mouse and the begen
shalar ar p children began to be
claiy and going to home and
the fox wase'nt greit chanpion
of caching mouse eniy more
The   End

Sample 6 Child D, Year 3, aged 7

Child D

Children C and D are both seven years old, but they have had very different experience. Child D is a seven-year-old boy who has had three years in the school. He is writing fluently but his work reflects his dependence on phonics. Thus his spelling is consistent with his incorrect pronunciations, e.g. 'closs' for 'cross' and 'shalap' for 'shut up'. He has some spelling conventions and punctuation to learn, as Sample 6 shows, and also uses the definite article inconsistently.

Child E

Child E is eight years old and is Child D's brother. His work in Sample 7 shows some progress in awareness of punctuation, although this and the indefinite article are used inconsistently.

Sample 7 Child E, Year 4, aged 8

Child F

Child F is a nine-year-old girl who has not been educated in Japan at all. She has been to school in the USA and British Forces Schools in Germany before joining Hillside recently. She enjoys much success in all aspects of schooling and, as Sample 8 shows, the errors in her work are as would be expected for an English-speaking child in a first draft.

Treasure Island

Maya and Nao was digging in the sand at the beach when they found a bag with a ring map and frizbee inside. The two of them looked at the map and found that it was a treasure map and the treasure map was showing the beach. Because it was near they decided to search for the treasure.

Unfortunately nearly every route had creatures which were guarding the treasure. They two of decided that they will take the short cut although they will meet a bull and an elephant.

They tiptoed along until a river was ahead of them. A suspension across it. The two of them crossed really scared to death. When they were at the end they jumped off and carried on with their journey. Suddenly a bull jumped out.

Nao threw his frizbee as hard as he could. The frizbee got in the bulls neck and the bull knocked out because it choked. As they walked on.... "Help —!?" "The the the there's an e.e.e. ELEPHANT!! And look! Its right ahead of us." said Maya staring at the map. Then the elephant began stumping towards them. "Help! its the end of our lives!" screamed the two. Suddenly it dropped dead. They walked fowarded..there was the treasure!

Sample 8 Child F, Year 4, aged 9

Chapter 10

Japanese Children at a Pre-Prep School

JULIE BUNKER

I am the head of the Pre-Prep Department at Crosfields School. Crosfields is a private day school for boys with just over 320 pupils. The Pre-Prep Department is in its fifth year and has grown from a department of 20 boys to over 80. Boys can start at the school when they are four and move to the Junior Department in the September following their seventh birthday. Over the years we have had a number of Japanese boys in the department. They have come from a many different backgrounds, with a range of different experiences. Generally, the things they have in common are that they come to us speaking little or no English, and that they spend only a limited time within the British education system before going somewhere else, often Japan.

At the moment we have two Japanese boys in the Pre-Prep. One is just four and has been with us for a term, and one is six and has been here for four terms. There is also a seven-year-old who spent nearly two years in the Pre-Prep Department before moving on to the Junior Department, and a few older boys.

When the boys initially come to Crosfields, obviously our first tasks are to integrate them into the system and teach them to communicate with their peers. The other boys are very helpful, and will talk to them, play with them and look after them. Sometimes it needs to be explained to the English boys that they need to speak clearly and carefully, but in a normal manner. I had one boy in my class who started to talk to his Japanese friend with a Japanese accent! The Japanese boys learn much of their language from being with their peers — sometimes they understand more English than they let on, and they do not always speak as much as they could. They rarely participate in discussions and initially find it difficult to listen to stories or to class explanations about a lesson.

We teach the Japanese to read the same way that we teach the other boys — they have a series of flashcards to learn before they start the reading scheme. Generally they learn these very quickly. Prior to starting the scheme they have picture books which are used to help them begin to develop their vocabulary. Alongside this they learn a sound a week to help them with both reading and writing. They seem to find the mechanical skills involved with learning to read very easy to assimilate, and so their mechanical reading progresses quite rapidly, at the same rate or even more quickly than that of their peers. However, they find it difficult to discuss the text or to predict what may happen next, as their command of the spoken language does not allow them this freedom. Similar problems occur in their written work, as they are able to write isolated words but find sentence construction difficult. Even when they have grasped the rudiments of English grammar, we find they tend to leave out words when writing, or to use words in the wrong order. The following are examples:

- In Jalal house game and tent.
- I see Alice in Wonderland everyone see Alice Wonderland and back at house is my birthday party today and chocolate cake and eat chocolate cake is very nice cakes.

These two pieces of writing were produced by the same child, the second about a month later than the first. He is a six-year-old boy who has been in school for four terms and he wrote them unaided. He knew what he wanted to say, but there are a number of words missing.

Some of the boys receive extra help with their work if this is deemed necessary. This is not restricted to the Japanese children — any children, whether they are English, Asian, European or Japanese, get the same opportunities. However, if a Japanese boy starts at Crosfields later in his school life, say at the age of six, or is not making the progress we might have expected, then he is given individual help on a regular basis. It is also important that they do not forget too much during a holiday so, again, some regular individual help with language is advantageous.

We find the Japanese are good at spelling with the older boys being able to spell quite complicated words, but not unexpectedly perhaps, not so good at creative writing, where they have not only got to develop their ideas in an imaginative way, but also express them in a language which they cannot speak fluently and about which they are not confident.

In many ways we find it easier to teach the Japanese boys maths and we have had a number of boys who have been gifted in this area. Obviously, the younger they are the easier it is, as explanations are usually simple and they can grasp what they have to do from watching other people. As they get older it can become more complicated, depending on their understanding of English — if there is a concept they do not understand they can find it hard to explain what the problem is, and the explanations themselves get more difficult for them to understand. Maths of course is a very broad subject, and it is the mechanical operations which they find easiest. Investigations, problem solving and areas that require greater use of language may be more difficult. However, as I said earlier, they generally seem to find maths and areas of the curriculum which deal mainly with facts easier than ones where language is a key element, and they achieve better results.

Of course, different Japanese children learn at different rates, as do all children. Some of them have a natural desire to want to communicate with staff and boys, and to make progress with their work, whereas others are much quieter and need more encouragement and individual help. Some of the boys also use lack of understanding of the language to their advantage when there is something they do not want to do! However slowly or quickly their acquisition of language is progressing, the thing it needs most is practice. Here there are a number of factors that need to be taken into account — the child's desire to learn and his willingness to 'have a go', as well as opportunities for using English outside the school situation. Most Japanese parents are keen for their children to achieve a good standard in all areas of the curriculum and they want to help them with their work. However, some of them are not confident enough in their use and understanding of English to help their children with their English language development.

In conclusion then, the academic achievement of Japanese boys of this age is quite often on a level with that of their peers, in some areas if not all. The areas that are usually weakest are those of free, creative, imaginative or descriptive writing. However, individual achievement varies greatly, as one has to take into consideration a number of factors which will have an effect on the child's rate of progress. These include their natural aptitude and their character, as well as the degree to which their language skills have developed.

Chapter 11

The View of a Second Language Specialist Working for an Education Support Service

SARAH MITCHELL

Introduction

I work for a team of 10 full- and part-time staff who give support in Local Education Authority schools where there are just one or two bilingual pupils. In schools where there are many bilingual students there may be a full-time language teacher from another team in Multicultural Services. Our team provides support once or twice a week to the children and staff in the school. At the moment the 10 of us are working in 50 schools. These are the outlying schools all around the County of Berkshire. We tend not to be in the schools in the middle of the big towns but in smaller places like Lambourne, Ascot and village schools as well.

We meet many Japanese children, although we work with children from all over the world, most whom are here temporarily. Over the last few years there has been an increase in the number of Japanese families and at one point last year there were Japanese children in 22% of our schools. We have noticed that there have been similar concerns and questions from the mainstream staff in schools, so recently we made it a part of our staff development to learn more about the Japanese education system and about the needs of the children when they come into this country.

Problems Encountered by Japanese Children

I shall deal specifically with some of the difficulties encountered by the Japanese children in our outlying schools. There are many similar problems experienced by Japanese children and other bilingual children but there were some that are encountered specifically by Japanese children.

Isolation

Many Japanese families do not live near other Japanese families. The fathers are working long hours so it is left to the mother to be responsible for the care and education of the children. These mothers often feel isolated. In many cases they are newly arrived and do not feel confident speaking English and consequently they do not feel comfortable coming into the schools and talking to teachers.

Length of stay

The second point is that many of the bilingual children I work with are here for fairly short periods of time, usually no more than two years, whereas many Japanese children are here for up to five years. This could be a significant part of their education and can make a big difference because if children return to their home country within two years they remember the system in that country. The long-stay children, however, may have never been to school in Japan and the whole of their primary education may have been in this country.

High expectations

Japanese families, we have found, always have high expectations for their children. They want them to do well in both English and Japanese schools, because how well they do in this country determines how well they will do in Japan. These children feel great pressure, especially at the secondary school level. They have a lot of homework from their English school and also from their Japanese Saturday School, and there may be conflict between which studies take precedence. They work very hard. There is no Japanese school in Berkshire, so the children have to spend time travelling to London at the weekend.

Lack of knowledge about the two education systems

Before we had our own in-service training we found lack of knowledge on both sides. We did not know about the Japanese system and Japanese parents knew very little about our system. They are different and there are different philosophies and approaches. For instance, a Japanese parent coming into one of our primary schools, might remark on how like a Japanese kindergarten it is, because the children sit in groups and not in rows. This may have a subconscious effect on whether their children value this education, or respond as if it is just kindergarten education for a junior-aged child. To assist with this concern we have now begun to explain our approach. If the mother does not speak enough English we need to get the philosophy of our education system put into Japanese and this is one of the things we are doing at the moment. What we do have is a paper that we give to the schools about the Japanese education system and some of the difficulties Japanese children might encounter coming into our schools.

Emphasis on spoken English

The lack of emphasis on speech in Japanese schools has been mentioned several times elsewhere in this volume. We do find that many Japanese children find it difficult to adapt to our kind of approach. It causes concern to teachers because within our education system children are assessed on spoken English. If they have been here for six months prior to the National Standard Assessment Tests in years 2, 6, and 9, they are going to be assessed on their speaking skills. If they are reluctant to speak, the assessment will not look very good. On the other hand, children who have not been to school in Japan do not have this problem. If they have been through our system when they come into primary school they tend to settle quickly and make excellent progress. But I wonder how they will feel going back to Japan and the different approach there — whether they are going to be asked to be quiet!

Relevance of our advice to parents

Another aspect of our job is to give advice to parents on how they can help their children with English at home. I have found that the standard advice is not appropriate. For instance we suggest they have English-speaking children home to play after school and in the holidays, but if the mother speaks limited English, and the child has to go home to Japanese studies, there is not a lot of time for play. We also suggest they watch some good English children's television but Japanese parents say that if they were going to find the time to watch television they would rather watch a Japanese video. We have therefore had to adapt our advice to make it appropriate and relevant for a Japanese family.

Conclusion

Finally, Japanese children seem to do very well in our education system but I feel that these children often feel disoriented because they are not working in a system which they are accustomed to. Mainstream teaching staff in the upper primary and lower secondary schools are concerned about this and welcome suggestions on how to overcome this disorientation.

Chapter 12

Do's and Don'ts in Bilingual Education

MO PICKERING

I do not wish to repeat the points already made by Sarah Mitchell in the previous chapter, but support teachers at our Japanese Resources Centre are dealing with a situation similar to hers. We work as peripatetic teachers in British schools which have Japanese pupils attending. I want to mention four key areas.

Access to the Curriculum

Firstly, I am concerned with access to the curriculum. The priority is that the children are learning. It does not matter ultimately whether they first learn certain things in English or Japanese. There are simply certain things they need to know. They need to develop concepts appropriately for their age and their general stage of learning. In their understanding of geography, for example, can they use a map? Are they developing special skills? If they are learning about electricity, they need to know that electricity is powerful and that it is both useful and potentially dangerous. If they can be taught using English that they can understand, this will build up their facility in the language; but, whether they learn the key points in English or in Japanese, the important thing is that their conceptual development is continuing.

Access to the curriculum is very important. There have been many upheavals in the English National Curriculum in the past few years and at one stage I was very worried because any mention of the issue of bilingualism seemed to have been dropped from the documentation. It was not recognised that this was a separate need; so teachers were left with a choice of looking at Japanese children either in the mainstream classroom or under the heading of special needs. We know that their linguistic need is not the same as a learning need. They are quite capable of learning but

93

they do not have the language, at the moment, to express themselves or to absorb information fully. In the mean time, however, the issue of the needs of children using English as an Additional Language is now officially recognised again.

In-Class Support

Point number two is the need for in-class support. We focus as much as possible on sending our staff, most of whom can use Japanese as well as English, into mainstream classrooms. So the situation is not one of removing a child, opening them up and pouring in English and then returning them to the classroom. It does not work like that. Children can learn by other means: watching, copying their peers, thinking, using skills other than linguistic skills. It is not good to interrupt their general learning by removing them from their peer group. We give as much support as possible in the classroom and, when appropriate, some tightening up of certain areas of language. In that way the children are using English as a medium for learning something more interesting than the language alone.

Support for Mainstream Staff

The third area is support for mainstream staff in British schools. You often find that teachers in British schools are very well-meaning, very professional and very anxious to help Japanese children. Teachers are concerned about failing these children, and they need to be put at their ease if there are situations where they cannot stop the whole class to help one or two particular children.

On another issue, teachers' reactions can be passed on to their pupils, so they must be very careful about the way they respond to another culture; misunderstanding or unfamiliarity with certain cultural behaviour patterns, foods, or artwork can lead to an unguarded negative reaction from a class teacher which pupils may imitate. For example, I have seen a teacher spontaneously pull a disgusted face at the thought of eating octopus.

We can give mainstream teachers information about the education system in Japan and the parallels with ours, and about cultural similarities and differences. I think it is important that teachers are as informed as possible so that they both hold and foster a view of the pupils in their class (and their parents) as being, not better or worse, but different, and good.

The Peer Group Setting

The fourth issue is the peer group setting for the child. I think British teachers sometimes forget that a Japanese pupil, like any other person, will be different in different settings; they may see somebody who is shy, and not realise that when they are playing with their Japanese friends they are more bouncy and talkative. I think that needs to be remembered. The influence of the peer group on any child is extremely important. When we have the opportunity to do it, we go into schools before the Japanese child has actually arrived and do a session on Japanese culture. We let the British children ask questions and explain to them gently that, 'A child is coming in who can already write their name in English. Can anybody write their name in Japanese? Oh, then isn't it good that we have a person who can speak another language.' This sets the scene so that when Japanese children arrive they are perceived as different, but in a positive way, not better or worse. It also means that peer group respect feeds back to the Japanese child. And I try to find ways of showing that a Japanese child has a lot to offer to the English peer group.

Chapter 13

Observation of Japanese Pre-school Children as an Interlocutor

MICHELLE TURNER

I have been working at the University of Reading for the Japanese project, so I am not looking at the issues from a teacher's point of view. I have a Linguistics degree, and it is in language that my interest lies. While studying Linguistics I became interested in child language acquisition and second language learning and teaching. I was delighted when I was selected to participate as an Interlocutor on the University of Reading project, and my task was to elicit the English language from a young child who was a native speaker of Japanese. At the time he was three years and four months old. At the onset of the project he communicated purely in Japanese and watched television at home, usually English programmes, for about 20 hours a week.

For our first meeting we met in the Speech Clinic, which was an excellent venue because the rooms are sound proofed. This meant that you could obtain high quality recordings and the parents could sit in the adjacent room and monitor our progress through a one-way mirror without distracting the child or myself. The room was equipped with toys to put the child and myself at ease. We tried to create a very natural environment. In very early sessions I initiated all of the questions. I used tag questions, *yes-no* questions and *wh*-questions, and the response that I got was purely 'yes' or 'er' sounds, Japanese sentences, symbolic noises, periods of silence, or he just produced nouns. These nouns I believed at the time to be English, but subsequently I have discovered they are in fact Japanese. That is 'trakku' (truck), 'basu' (bus) or 'engine' which you use in Japanese, too.

Over two months later it became apparent that he was using less Japanese and these words were becoming more anglicised or English sounding. And as time progressed he began to use colours, numbers and adjectives, and he stopped producing Japanese utterances when he was communicating with me even though the minute he went back to his parents he was using Japanese. He did not appear to be producing verbs, and in an attempt to try to elicit these verbs we devised a small test. He had to perform several tasks such as 'put the pencil in the cup and the cup inside the box'. However, this activity appeared to cause some distress, possibly because it was a little premature. So we decided to revert to play because we could elicit more language through play than through artificially structured tasks.

This child is now attending school and it is possible to see a vast change in his development. In his production, he has started to produce determiners such as 'this' and 'that'. He is using verbs such as the verb 'be' and he has increased his noun content. His comprehension is also much improved, although right at the beginning his comprehension was better than his production.

I am also acting as an Interlocutor for two other young children at the Japanese School in London. These are a little girl who is five years old and attending school and a little boy who is four years old and not yet attending school. Both children have resided in this country longer than the first child I saw. They also produce large numbers of nouns, colours, numbers and phrases such as 'I don't know' and 'I don't like', but in addition they use verbs such as 'fall', 'rain' and 'fly', and they use the *-ing* form of the verb, as in 'flying', 'raining'. Again, we subjected the children to the same sort of test with verbs, and again it seemed to cause distress and they became quiet and withdrawn. So, we reverted to playing and the children continued to produce the nouns and carried on doing as well as they were prior to that test.

Finally, I will make just a few general points. Most of the children we worked with passed through a quiet stage and a whispering stage. All of them have had good comprehension, practically from the beginning. Verbs appeared to be developing quite late. I would just like to say that it has been an immense pleasure working with these youngsters, just to watch them grow and develop, and I hope I can continue to do so for a long time. I am very grateful to the parents and children for being so cooperative.

Part 4: Views of Japanese Saturday School Teachers and Parents

Chapter 14

Roles and Responsibilities, and the Special Context of the Japanese Saturday School

EMIKO FURUYA-WISE

It has been my privilege to work with the children in the primary division of the Japanese Saturday School in London and to observe their learning. I would like to express my views on the Saturday School where I work as a part-time teacher. My discussion will concentrate on the following three perspectives: firstly, factors affecting what and how to teach the children at the school; secondly, the teacher's responsibilities and roles; and thirdly, suggestions for, and visions of the Japanese Saturday School in the future.

Factors Affecting What and How to Teach

I would first like to draw attention to the enormous pressure the teachers are under to make pupils' school attendance worthwhile, at the same time as ensuring that their Japanese language development does not fall behind. We make every effort to give the pupils self-confidence to acquire learning skills and regularly assign homework. In addition, we, as teachers, also have to have self-motivation for our own personal development. The four factors outlined below affect *what* and *how* we teach at the Japanese Saturday School.

The complexity of the learning environment

We have to take the issue of the school context into consideration; the situation of Japanese schools located in the UK is different from that of schools located in Japan. It should be obvious that extra time and consideration is required on the part of the teachers to deal with cultural and social aspects in general, ranging from social skills (school codes, rules and manners), traditional customs, social values, to an understanding of the context when pupils read text in Japanese. In class, some children need to be taught to adjust to Japanese classroom discipline.

Limited class time to cover the content of the Japanese national curriculum

As has already been mentioned by Kazue Aizawa in Chapter 2, considerably fewer teaching hours are allocated for the pupils at the Japanese Saturday School than the recommended time for pupils in Japan. In order to cope with such an adverse situation, not only does effective learning become essential in class, but there is also a heavy burden of homework.

Mixed language abilities

At the Japanese Saturday School, grouping of the pupils is based on their ages, as in Japan, and not on their Japanese language ability. Consequently, ability in Japanese is highly diverse in each class. Yet teachers are expected to teach the required content of the national curriculum. This is something which we have found very difficult to carry out.

Diversity in children's background

As indicated above, there is enormous diversity and complexity in the background of the pupils in one and the same class. Such diversity is caused by differences in the following areas:

- parents' nationalities (both are Japanese, or one parent is Japanese);
- parents' employment (Japanese, British or international companies);
- length of residence in the UK;
- choice of local school (state, independent or international school);
- location of school (located in rural or urban areas);
- degree of immersion into the community (well immersed or isolated);
- amount of extra-curricular activities;
- parents' views on what is important in their children's education (internationalisation; benefits from British education; Japanese language; conforming to the Japanese system; individual personal development);
- reasons for parents sending children to the Japanese Saturday School (for socialisation; for conformity to the Japanese education system; for the maintenance of culture; for acquiring Japanese literacy).

I have pointed out four factors which make teaching at the Japanese Saturday School particularly difficult. We are nevertheless making especial efforts to overcome such difficulties. Such measures will be discussed below.

Teachers' Responsibilities and Roles

We as teachers also need to integrate the individual pupils' learning requirements and needs into the classroom and to deliver the curriculum effectively. The following three points should be addressed in relation to this issue: first, children's well-being, personal development and communication needs; second, the development of Japanese language and literacy; and third, homework.

Children's well-being, personal development and communication needs

The school needs to be a happy place. The pupils are 'learning to learn at school'. We have to know their needs so that we can encourage them and give them confidence. They can then learn to enjoy achieving their targets. We always ask ourselves questions such as 'Is s/he happy at the Saturday School?'; 'Is s/he benefiting from the school?'; 'Is s/he happy to speak in Japanese with friends and teachers?'; 'Is s/he enjoying the school environment — people, facilities, events, etc.'; 'Does s/he have a sense of belonging to the class?'; 'Is s/he coping with the new environment and coping with the local school s/he attends?'

All these personal factors affect the pupils' interest in learning for better or worse. It is not easy in reality to practice this 'concern-contact-consider-communicate-continue' process, as responding to each child's needs in the class. Nevertheless, it is a teacher's role to make sure that learning takes place as effectively as possible.

Japanese language and literacy development

It is necessary for teachers at the Saturday School to plan effective activities for learning the content of the curriculum and to deliver these in class while still responding to the children's needs. These activities include learning Japanese through government approved textbooks. The teachers are required to complete the structurally graded textbooks for each age level in one year, going through them chapter by chapter without missing important content, so that at the end of the school year the children can be promoted to classes of the same level as full-time schools in Japan.

The government-approved textbooks have been designed so that new *Kanji* characters (Chinese script) are introduced at the rate of six to seven a week for children of eight and nine years old. The children need to keep up with this pace; otherwise their reading level will be affected. To keep up with their practice of *Kanji*, their reading comprehension and writing of sentences in the textbooks, pupils are expected to learn at home, using material given out in the classroom.

Homework

There are certain learning activities recommended for pupils at primary school level to do regularly at home. These include reading the textbook aloud, learning *Kanji* characters and copying sentences from the textbook. Assignments with graded objectives are given each week to the pupils. General practice in reading and writing in Japanese outside the context of the textbook is also encouraged in various ways.

Constant monitoring of the pupils' progress is a particularly heavy burden for a one-day-a-week part-time teacher. However, we cannot overstate the value of giving extra time and effort to maintain continuity for the class, linking Saturday to Saturday by monitoring the pupils' learning progress at home and giving the right encouragement for individual development, as well as effective planning of class activities. Our work often involves preparing materials in order to suit particular learning skills and content. This requires careful consideration and skill so that the individual's level is catered for.

Overview and Suggestions for the Future

Finally, I would like to express my views on the role of the Japanese Saturday School and cooperation between the school, the Japanese community in the UK and the Japanese government, i.e. the Japanese Ministry of Education.

Overview of the Japanese Saturday School in London

The main objective of the Japanese Saturday School is to maintain pupils' Japanese language development so that they are ready to fit into the school system in Japan at any time. It is a fee-paying private school, and it is a part of the Japanese School Ltd administered by a group of businessmen on a one-year rota representing Japanese companies. The history of the Japanese Saturday School dates back to 1970 when it started in a rented London office room with hired teachers and a small group of children. Currently, there are six full-time non-teaching staff who are on three-year leave from state schools in Japan. The teaching staff consists of people with various qualifications and experiences.

Suggestions on the school's role in responding to children's needs

In order to help pupils with their education, I would suggest that the school should take an active role in responding flexibly to various needs. There should be, for example, an open structure enabling the people concerned to be consulted on its organisation, regulations and practices. There should also be a structured staff career development programme, and it would be desirable if there were support from specialists to improve coordination between the Saturday School, local schools and the pupils' families.

The role of the Japanese community in the UK and the Japanese Government

I would also suggest that the Japanese community in the UK and the Japanese government should support Japanese-speaking children in the UK regardless of their parents' occupation and background. I hope that there will be public provision for bilingual language development and cultural education (not as commercialised provision) for children irrespective of age. It is also to be hoped that support for various research projects on language development and education will be provided by both the community and the government.

Chapter 15

Some Issues about Becoming Bilingual

KAZUE AIZAWA

Unlike Emiko Furuya-Wise in the previous chapter, I have mostly been teaching older students aged 14, 15 and 16. In our lessons at the Saturday School the emphasis tends to be on reading, writing and comprehension rather than on speaking. This is especially true of the older students. We are also expected to follow the normal Japanese curriculum, and we are supposed to do that on 40 Saturdays, that is, 80 hours a year. So we have to cram our students with knowledge, as they are required to know as much as normal students in Japan.

Several of the chapters in this volume have mentioned interactive teaching. When I reflect on my own method of teaching, I realise that it is very far from interactive. It tends to be cramming. This is partly deliberate and partly unavoidable because that is what we teachers are expected to do, and that is what Japanese children normally experience. For the older students the main problem is how to find the time to study Japanese after they have finished all the work they are supposed to do at their normal Monday-to-Friday schools. Also at this level they have to start thinking about British GCSEs and A Levels.

My students talk about 'black Fridays' as it is on Friday night that they prepare for their Japanese lessons on Saturday morning. I expect my students to spend at least three or four hours preparing for a lesson. Quite a few students stay up until two or three o'clock in the morning, preparing for their next day. Some students manage; a few manage magnificently but, inevitably, others do not and I think that we have to face the reality that some students simply cannot juggle two sets of school work at a time. There are some students who return to Japan after a few years in this country with imperfect English and imperfect Japanese. I have come across some cases like this.

The most important thing for students of this age group is their own motivation. And in motivating students an important factor is the parents' attitude. When the parents are academically minded and are firmly convinced their children have to have a good command of Japanese, then the children, too, tend to be highly motivated and they work hard and they usually succeed.

I sometimes hear Japanese parents say that their son or daughter has recently made great progress in English, but that, as a result, his/her Japanese has deteriorated. But in my experience, this is rarely the case. Although I am not a specialist, it seems to me that after the initial period of 12 months or so, there is a clear correlation between a student's ability in English and that in Japanese. In most cases, children who do well at their English schools do well also at the Japanese School. I think this is more or less a universal phenomenon.

The top students at the Saturday School are as good as, if not better than, those at normal schools in Japan. However, when I compare my students with their counterparts in Japan, one weakness I find in my students is the quality of their vocabulary. Of course, most children who come from Japanese families speak Japanese at home, so they have quite sufficient Japanese for day-to-day conversation. But when it comes to more formal, literary vocabulary, they tend to be a little weak. Quite often they cannot use difficult or sophisticated words properly even when they know what those words mean. Perhaps this is because they are not used to seeing them used in normal contexts.

Speaking of vocabulary, I have noted a quite interesting phenomenon in bilingual students. Some of our students at the Japanese School have recently arrived from Japan, but others have been brought up almost exclusively in this country. So they are supposed to be truly bilingual. I remember giving private lessons to such a girl, who was born and brought up in the Philippines and then came to England. She was educated almost completely in English, though, of course, her Japanese was quite fluent, too. She was preparing for a Japanese A Level, and the Japanese A Level examination consists mostly of Japanese–English translations. When we were doing some translation exercises, she came across the word 'philosophy', and she was unable to translate it into Japanese. I told her the Japanese for 'philosophy', which is *tetsugaku*. What surprised me was that she already knew that word and what it meant, but it did not occur to her that 'philosophy' and *tetsugaku* mean one and the same thing. This is a phenomenon I often observe in bilingual children. It is as though there were two separate compartments in their head without a communicating door in between. They have an adequate set of English words and an adequate set of Japanese words, but they cannot really match one with the other. So they seem to find it difficult to interpret or translate from English to Japanese or from Japanese to English. I do not know how linguists or psychologists explain this phenomenon, but I do find it interesting.

Chapter 16

Differences in Cultural and Linguistic Expectations between Britain and Japan

MARIKO SASAGAWA-GARMORY

A good pupil in Japan may become a bad one in a British classroom. Perhaps a Japanese child who comes to an English school feels that he or she is stepping into a very different world like Alice in Wonderland. As I have worked at a high school and a junior high school in Japan and have been a private teacher in England, I would like to explore the differences by comparing the two cultures.

In Japan, as classes contain 30 to 40 pupils, they sit still, listen to the teacher and make notes. They seldom ask questions or express their opinions. If they do so, they are thought to be showing off, and people who do that are not liked in Japanese society. However, in the UK their quiet, good Japanese attitude appears too passive to English teachers and they struggle to understand what Japanese pupils are thinking.

Japanese students face problems not only in speaking and listening, but also in writing and reading. Discussion and projects are very rare in Japan — pupils are encouraged more to memorise facts and they are tested to see if their knowledge is accurate. Even if they started to learn English as a compulsory subject in Japan at the age of 13, they may not write more than two short sentences because it would be an enormous job for teachers to correct 30 to 40 compositions and mark them. Therefore, the students do not know how to collect the necessary information, build up chapters and develop paragraphs. They usually have difficulties in carrying out research in geography, science and history. They are astonished to know that even in maths they have to explain the equations instead of just solving problems. They need time to get used to thinking for themselves and organising their project work.

With regard to other aspects of school culture, they are bewildered when they are told to sit down on the carpet on the floor, wearing shoes. In Japan we take off outdoor shoes inside the building and change them. Moreover, when girls are told to sit cross-legged, they hesitate because that sort of style is for boys in Japan. It is not girl-like and they would be scolded at home if they did this.

After doing mathematical calculations, the class is told the right answers. At this point, Japanese children will be totally confused because in Japan '√' (a tick) means that something is wrong. They are used to being given 'O' (circle) when the answer is right. Moreover, sometimes 'yes' and 'no' mean the opposite to English. Japanese use of 'yes' and 'no' depends on whether you agree with what the other person has said. So if you use negative questions such as, 'Aren't you going to eat that?' to children who don't want to eat any more, they may respond with 'Yes.' What they mean is, 'Yes, I agree with you — I'm not going to eat that'. Negative statements or statements followed by a tag question may evoke the same kind of unexpected response. So if you say to an only child, 'You don't have a brother, do you?', he or she may reply 'Yes', meaning, 'You're right. I don't have a brother'.

In addition, the Japanese are afraid of expressing different opinions from others. Instead, they try to harmonise with people. Therefore they find it difficult to say 'no' to others. On the other hand, if someone says 'no' to them, they are ashamed and hurt. For example, a little Japanese boy who was beginning to understand English plucked up the courage to say, 'See you tomorrow!' to his teacher. However, her reply was, 'No, not tomorrow. See you on Monday!' Since he had expected to be praised with a smile, he was devastated and he did not want to go to the English nursery any more. Certainly, he was being too sensitive, but Japanese children need more smiles and encouragement than English children do.

In Chapter 7 Asako Yamada-Yamamoto suggested that Japanese pupils take more time to master English because of the different word order. My experience has also been that they struggle to find suitable verbs at the top part of the sentence instead of at the end as in Japanese, putting a long pause after the subjects. Another problem is articles. The Japanese language does not have articles, and both singular and plural forms are the same for Japanese nouns. So often, articles and plural forms are omitted in Japanese children's compositions. Though I have been in the UK for 10 years, when I make a shopping list, I still only write the name of items in the singular, for example 'apple' and 'egg'. My husband always teases me for my typical Japanese mistakes. The Japanese language and culture are very different. It is therefore important to give extra time to Japanese children in class. Once they master English, their diligence will help them to catch up with the others.

Lastly, in Japan if parents make some comment about the teaching, they are thought to be rude, so they do not express their opinions or ask questions. So it is essential to encourage the parents as well as children to be in contact with teachers. However, from my point of view, the parents have to change their expectations towards English school, teachers and their own children, too. The parents want their children to improve their English but they also hope they keep their Japaneseness. They should bear in mind that their children are studying at British schools. Real cooperation between English teachers and Japanese parents could support Japanese children and make it easier for them to adjust to British schools.

Chapter 17

Initial Experiences at a British School: A Mother's Account

YUMIKO SHIBATA

I am writing this chapter as a mother of two Japanese boys who have been attending local English schools. I will not therefore address academic topics like some of the other contributors. However, what I can do here is to narrate our own personal experiences of a new educational system.

First of all, I would like to take this opportunity to say a massive 'thank you' to the people who have been involved in crucial research about Japanese children. I believe that this kind of research is desperately needed not only for Japanese families, but also teachers, carers, friends and all the people who are concerned with our children as there is no doubt that it could help to make our experiences much easier, happier and more worthwhile.

Let me explain why we have been in Britain. Three years ago we learned that we would have to move to London and stay for a while because of my husband's job. The first thing we had to consider was about our elder son's education. At that time, he was six years old and had just finished his kindergarten in Japan. Unfortunately he had no idea about London, no knowledge of English except a few words like 'Hello', 'Thank you' or 'Bye'. In addition to that, neither I nor my husband had any experience of living in a foreign country, and it was very difficult to get enough information about the British educational system. You can imagine how much we worried about it. However, we decided to let him go to the local school and managed to find a small independent school, which had plenty of experience in accepting Japanese children.

However, I must point out that we had another choice at that time. He could have got a place in the Japanese Daily School in London, if we had wanted. There the children can study from Monday to Friday in almost the same way as at home in Japan, with the same textbooks and Japanese-speaking teachers. It is much easier for children to settle down and their parents seem less worried about their future when they go back to Japan. Then why did we let him go to a local school, not the Japanese Daily School? I would like to point out three reasons for our decision. Firstly, we thought that it would be a precious opportunity for him to learn about the culture, history, life-styles and customs, of Britain. Secondly, he could take advantage of the opportunity to have a fine command of English, which has become a worldwide language nowadays, and which seemed absolutely vital for his future. Thirdly, anybody we had consulted about this matter said to us, 'Don't worry! Children, especially young children like yours, will have no problems. I'm sure that he will speak English fluently very soon.' So we simply believed what they said.

Now I have found that the latter was not true. As far as I know, any Japanese children attending local schools have difficulties to a greater or lesser degree, and huge amounts of effort, time, patience, love, tears, and support would definitely be behind the success stories. Presumably, people who return to Japan would not want to talk about bad experiences, or they are so busy settling down to a new life that they have no time to look back. Nonetheless, we need to face the problems and try to solve them. Otherwise the situation will never improve for our children.

As I have mentioned already, my elder son could not speak any English at first. Despite this, he seemed to look forward to meeting his new friends and teachers on his very first day at his new school in Britain. What he did when he was introduced to his teacher was to say 'Hello' and bow deeply at the same time, which was a mixture of English and Japanese customs and made me giggle. Even though I left the school, having followed her advice, everything reminded me of him and the rest of the day seemed like a month or two. When it was time to collect him, I found my poor boy sleeping in the middle of the classroom while other children were enjoying story time! I could imagine how exhausted he was.

However, surprisingly, he dressed in his school uniform next morning and urged me to take him to school. We were delighted to know that he liked his new school so much. But our happiness did not last long.

On the third day, I got an unexpected phone call and was told to meet the headmistress that afternoon. It did not sound like good news at all. At the meeting, I just could not believe my ears to hear that my boy's behaviour was so appalling that many children were frightened of him. The headmistress also said that my boy was always shouting in a loud voice and kicking or punching. I could hardly believe it because he had never done such things before. She warned me that a school was a place where all the children were supposed to study and not a place for such violent games.

No sooner had I picked up my boy than I asked him about these incidents. After admitting it rather innocently, he said to me, 'I don't know why nobody understood what I said'. Apparently he had spoken to them in Japanese all day long. But soon he realised that some of his classmates called him 'Karate Man'. So he started to behave like that in order to please them and attract their attention. 'I didn't mean to hurt anybody, Mum. I just wanted to make friends', he added. I suggested to him that it was wrong to do that and that he should have been kind to them as usual and tried to pick up their words. He agreed with me very sadly. Then I wrote a letter to the headmistress, explaining what he had thought and what he had promised. At the same time, I questioned whether three days were long enough for children to master the new language. As I could not bear my boy to be considered rough because of his lack of communication skills, I asked the staff to allow more time so that he could learn the new language and settle down in his new environment.

In spite of my poorly written English, the headmistress wrote back to me immediately, saying how much she was moved by my letter and gave me an apology for her quick judgement without considering my son's background. I was also touched by her sympathy and felt that our decision had not been wrong. I decided to cooperate with the school as much as I could.

What I learned through this incident was how important it is for parents and teachers to trust each other and maintain good relationships. Presumably this would not be a problem for the English-speaking parents. However, we are likely to fail because of an inadequate command of English.

Fortunately, no other serious problems developed at that school, and gradually my son showed an improvement in English which was achieved by the dedicated staff who provided intensive teaching and warm encouragement, and by his friends who were very kind to him. Soon all his classmates experienced his good nature and so did the teachers. One year later, his English became good enough to pass the seven plus exam, which seemed very competitive to me, and now he has been attending a school for older boys for two years.

Nevertheless, our worries seem endless in spite of his good English because of our lack of knowledge about the National Curriculum, and lack of enough up-to-date information about his school. I find it very difficult to appreciate how much he can understand, what he has studied, how the boys are behaving at school, and how my son is coping with his friends, especially as the issue of bullying seems to be one of the most serious problems in the UK as well. In addition, most Japanese families tend to be in a dilemma because teachers of local schools suggest to us that our children should be immersed in English language and culture as much as possible, while Japanese teachers at the Saturday School emphasise how difficult it is for our children to maintain their own language and culture without our consistent support. How can we do both?

On the other hand, we do not have to worry about my younger son, who is now four years old. That is because he had plenty of time to prepare himself before going to a local school. Besides, we have more knowledge and experience than we had three years ago. What is more, our improved English helps us greatly to find friends and the information we need. Therefore, we can feel more relaxed and predict what sort of things might happen to him. From my point of view, obviously younger children seem more adaptable and flexible than older children.

To return to my elder son who is nine now and being required to achieve at a higher level and whose situation is getting more complicated and difficult, I cannot help heaving a big sigh, because we are feeling so insecure about what will happen to him. One of the teachers I talked with said that she felt as if she were walking in the dark jungle. That is exactly the same feeling as I have, because we have not got any maps, or compasses, or guides or torches. Nobody seems to know where we are going or how long we will have to wait, especially when the children are still silent, or what is the best method to find the right way. Nevertheless, I have been totally inspired to learn that so many people have been working for our children, caring for our children and loving our children. How lucky they are to be provided with a wonderful opportunity to study in a marvellous multicultural environment with such great support. I am quite convinced that not only the language, but also both the bitter and sweet experiences they have had will be a treasure for the whole of their lives. This will be a challenge for themselves and their parents.

Part 5: Learning and Teaching Other Languages

Chapter 18

Reading and Writing in Japanese: A Challenging Task

HELEN GILHOOLY

I am the Co-ordinator of Derbyshire County Council's Japanese Resources Centre, established six years ago in response to the building of the Toyota factory in the area. The Centre has three main roles: to give English Language Support to Japanese pupils in mainstream British schools; to teach Japanese to British secondary school pupils; and to develop school materials related to Japanese studies.

I am not going to discuss the English language support we give to our Japanese children because this has already been dealt with earlier in Chapter 12 by my colleague, Mo Pickering. Instead I will give some thoughts from the viewpoint of a British person teaching Japanese to British pupils.

One point I would like to make is that Japanese at beginner's level does not have to be a difficult language to learn. At least in terms of speaking and listening, once the student has become accustomed to certain differences such as sentence order and points of pronunciation, learning is quite a straightforward process. My students often comment that Japanese is easier than French because the verb is not conjugated, there is no masculine/feminine, no plural and so forth. Where difficulties do arise, it is in the teaching and learning of the Japanese writing system. I have experienced some obstacles in teaching the Japanese script to my students. They need to learn a number of symbols and Chinese characters each week. If they do not keep up with this it becomes increasingly difficult for them to participate in class activities, and they may become de-motivated. On the other hand, many students enjoy the challenge of learning a different script and it is important that the teacher keeps this enthusiasm going.

Therefore, although speaking Japanese can be fairly straightforward at beginner's level, the reading and writing of Japanese offers extra hurdles to the learner which do not have to be overcome when learning a European language. This difficulty is compounded by the content of the two main school examinations in this country, the General Certificate of Secondary Education (GCSE) and Advanced level (A Level). Both put a particular emphasis on reading and writing skills, although a speaking test will be added to the GCSE from 1998 to bring it in line with the National Curriculum, and it will be part of a final grade.

One solution to this would be to lengthen the time in which students learn Japanese, but this may not be possible on all school timetables and thus may limit further the number of schools able to offer Japanese to GCSE and A Level. (This parallels the situation of Japanese children learning Japanese at Saturday Schools in this country. They are limited by time because they have to keep up with their counterparts in Japan.)

A further point is that of motivation. Learning Japanese has a particular attraction to many students because it is 'different', and it is interesting to note that many of the schools in this country applying for Language School status have cited Japanese as one of the languages they will commit themselves to teaching. There is also an increase of interest in the Derby area because of the location of the Toyota factory and other related Japanese companies which have heightened awareness and interest in Japan.

Added to these factors, there is the advantage of smaller groups, which keeps students' interest and motivation going. Typically, a pupil may learn French in a group of 25 to 30, but learn Japanese in a group of 6 to 15. Students are therefore able to receive and ask for more attention, and a range of ability can be more easily taught within one small group.

Chapter 19

Japanese and English: Languages of Different Organisation

LYDIA MOREY

I was brought up in Japan and educated in Japanese schools through the medium of Japanese until I was 15 years old, so I have the opposite experience of the children we are discussing in this volume. My background is that I received all of my compulsory education in Nagano prefecture in Japan, before returning to the UK for Ordinary and Advanced Level examinations, my degree and a Postgraduate Certificate in Education (PGCE). I cannot remember a time when I was not bilingual between English and Japanese.

I did have a very bad 'culture shock' experience when I first came to the UK. This was because, although when we were in Japan we had always talked about England as 'home', in fact culturally this was not the case for me. Even today my instinctive thought patterns are often Japanese. For example, when I think how I should relate to certain people I tend to apply the Japanese concepts of '*giri*' and '*on*' (social obligation). In this way I tend to expect relationships to be based on a Japanese model, and I consciously have to stop myself and reason that what I am expecting is the Japanese way of behaving and not an English one.

I now teach Japanese, and I could not agree more with what Helen Gilhooly has already presented in the previous chapter. I mainly teach sixth-formers, so the pupils I teach are older than those Helen Gilhooly teaches. I most often teach a one- or two-year beginners' course, often leading up to General Certificate of Secondary Education (GCSE) but occasionally leading to A Level, and here I shall address the issue of what foreign learners of Japanese find difficult. The first difficulty is the pupils' lack of knowledge about language in general — they are lacking basic concepts of how languages operate. For example, Japanese sends its verbs to the end of the sentence, but most pupils have never encountered the idea that SVO (Subject-Verb-Object) is not the only way a language can be organised. Thus I cannot start with the idea that in Japanese the verb goes at the end of the sentence, but rather I have to start one step further back with the concept that English is just one example of how a language can be organised, and it does not have to be like this. I am not trying to argue the case here for the teaching of grammar, but I would see some general knowledge about language as helpful to pupils.

For learners of Japanese at the beginners' level, particles seem to be one of the specific difficulties. This is partly to do with the fact that the Japanese particle marks grammatical functions, so to pupils who have no concept of grammar, it is difficult to use particles correctly. Another difficulty is the copula *'desu'* — at the very beginning of their study of Japanese, pupils use it quite happily and put it everywhere, but after a while they come to dislike the fact that it does not have one unique translation and its meaning covers everything from 'I am' to 'it is', and start to miss it off.

The worst thing about beginners' Japanese is probably the counting system — not only are two different counting systems used, but when you are using one of those, you have to put a 'counter' (or a classifier) onto the end of the word, depending on the shape of the object so that, for example, counting pieces of paper is different from counting pencils. My students often dislike this very strongly, partly because they do not see the need for it, and partly because what they spontaneously produce is incorrect. For example, within four weeks of starting Japanese I would have taught them the numbers and the sentence pattern *'Ani ga imasu'*. ('I have an elder brother'). The more able pupils will immediately put the two pieces of learning together and try to say things like *'Ni ani ga imasu'*, and they are very disappointed when I tell them that this is in fact incorrect, and that *'Ani ga futari imasu'* ('I have two elder brothers') is correct.

The final difficulty I would like to talk about is the script. I always introduce the script in lesson one, and try to avoid *romaji* if at all possible. I think that this is really the answer to the issue of script, because if the pupils do not ever see *romaji*, they find it easier to accept the way real Japanese is written by real Japanese people, and they just have to get on and learn it. Of course it is not always easy, particularly with the classes I only teach once a week. I find that I really need to be teaching them at least twice a week to see progress with the script. So if the pupils start writing in *romaji* I do not really approve, but I do not forbid it either, as that would make the classroom too uncomfortable for them. I find that students tend to split into two groups — those that love script and those who hate it. Those who love script are wonderful, because you give them a book and they will come back and have finished two or three chapters and find it satisfying and interesting. With those who hate script it is really hard work and one has constantly to keep plugging away at it.

I would like to bring up one issue that has not yet been referred to in this volume, and that is the issue of Japanese children who are sent from Japan without their parents, put into British private schools and told to get on with it. I do regularly get asked to go into private schools to teach Japanese children, and although the numbers I have seen are limited, there seems to be a significant minority of Japanese children who are being sent over here by their parents as a 'hiding' mechanism because they have failed in the Japanese education system. I would not like to overgeneralise the issue, but I have seen several cases of Japanese children in school over here whose background is not quite what the school was told by the parents on enrolment. It is often only through talking with the children in Japanese that I have discovered that they have failed entrance examinations, or that they have had social difficulties in fitting into Japanese schools, and I feel that there is an issue here in the children bringing these problems with them to the UK, while the school has not been given the full information to support such children adequately. I do feel fairly strongly that this is an issue that someone needs to address.

Finally, I have recently started to act as private tutor to several Japanese children in Cardiff, South Wales, who attend comprehensive schools during the week and the Japanese School on Saturdays. I have been helping them mainly with their English, but also with their other school subjects as well. I am beginning to find the differences in learning styles and expectations between the children's Japanese learning experiences and their British ones quite fascinating, and I hope that in the future I may have something worthwhile to contribute on the subject, too.

Chapter 20

A Different Language: A Source of Challenge and Enjoyment

KIYOKO ITO

Most of my clients are solicitors and accountants who have had a private school education. Most of them have good knowledge of a few European languages, so naturally they are confident in learning foreign languages. When they are offered language tuition, they choose Japanese because they are getting more and more opportunities to conduct businesses with Japanese clients. However, because Japanese is very different from European languages, learners, especially senior ones, may lose their confidence and motivation soon after starting Japanese lessons. They may have learnt Latin, French, German, Spanish or Italian, so they consider that Japanese is just another language. On the other hand, they are anxious to be excellent learners of the Japanese language.

Written Japanese is a real problem for most of them. However, they do enjoy learning *Hiragana*. Some are fascinated by the difference between alphabets and they show their enthusiasm in writing *Hiragana*. However, *Katatana* becomes a burden for them. *Kanji* is a totally new concept and they are capable of adopting some of *Kanji* within their own system. But *Kunyomi* (Japanese reading) and *Onyomi* (Chinese reading) are a cause of confusion or even desperation for them. Japanese grammar also seems to be very different from their expectations. So when they make a small mistake they make a fuss about it. They think they have been silly and they cannot bear to have made such a 'silly' mistake. On the other hand, people who have had difficulty in learning, for example, French in the past find pleasure in learning Japanese, since French and Japanese are entirely different. They love the difference.

At Central Foundation Boys' School I teach Japanese in Year 8 and Year 9. According to the school, my pupils have been identified as gifted linguists, but they do have difficulties and only half of the original participants survive after six months. The boys with ethnic origins in continents such as Asia and Africa seem to be the best learners, as they know both English and other languages which are not European. In addition, their level of interest in Japan makes a clear difference to their attitudes towards learning.

I also teach diplomats at the University of Westminster. Although they are very serious and hardworking learners, they say that they need plenty of time to understand Japanese. They learn about Japanese culture and customs at the same time and we often talk about Eastern philosophy, but acquiring another language is just like exploring a new world, and aspects that are not familiar in one's own language can seem rather odd. For example, one diplomat told me that he simply could not cope with Japanese classifiers such as *hitotsu, ikko, ichimai, ippon, issatsu* and *ichidai*.

I have an 8-year-old son and a 12-year-old daughter. They go to their father's country, Cyprus, and their mother's country, Japan, nearly every year. Turkish is no problem for them, but written Japanese is a real hazard. They go to the Japanese Saturday School but their homework is an impossible task to complete. Every Friday is a 'black Friday' for them. Having said that, they seem to enjoy a bit of *Kanji* and the atmosphere of the Japanese School.

Probably, for learners, their mental reward or satisfaction is not straightforward. They should think about time and goals. Setting goals is much easier if they have a clear idea of when they want to achieve them. Besides, the most important thing is that they spend a little time every day writing and reading Japanese. Some learners do Japanese before breakfast.

Chapter 21

Multilingual Classrooms

VIV EDWARDS

Introduction

People have always moved between countries, sometimes to colonise or trade, sometimes to find work or to improve their standard of living and, on other occasions, to escape famine or persecution. But the scale of population movement in the second half of the twentieth century has been particularly striking. By the late 1980s, one language 'census' discovered that over 170 different languages were spoken in London schools (ILEA, 1987).

British teachers have needed to respond to linguistic and cultural diversity in a range of ways. In the early stages, the main responsibility for meeting the needs of new arrivals fell on teachers of English as a second language in special reception centres (Edwards & Redfern, 1992). With the passing of time, there was growing dissatisfaction with this solution. The only English-speaking model in these 'withdrawal' classes was the teacher, and children therefore had no opportunity to interact with a range of fluent English speakers. Children also had restricted access to the curriculum and so fell further and further behind their English-speaking peers.

From the mid-1980s onwards, the prevailing wisdom has been that mainstream classrooms are the best place for new arrivals: because of the great emphasis placed in British schools on the role of talk in learning and the importance of collaborative learning, there is no shortage of English-speaking models; there are plenty of opportunities for real communication; there has also been a growing appreciation of the ways in which maths, science and other areas of the curriculum can support language learning. Teachers of English as a second language became language support teachers, working alongside class and subject teachers in the mainstream school.

The relationship between mainstream and language support teachers has often been a troubled one (Bourne, 1989). For instance, mainstream teachers have tended to rely too heavily on language support teachers and have often failed to take responsibility for the language learners in their classes. A belated attempt to address this question has taken the form of a government initiative called 'Meeting the needs of bilingual learners' which addresses the professional development needs of mainstream teachers. Many of the courses offered to teachers as part of this initiative concentrate on two main areas. The first addresses teachers' need to find out more about the children they are teaching. The second affects the kinds of classroom strategies which are likely to improve success in learning. As well as looking at specific English language teaching techniques, teachers are encouraged to explore ways of using children's experience of their home languages in the classroom.

Finding out about Children

'Monolingualism can be cured: learn another language', proclaims a Canadian poster which makes fun of the arrogant assumptions of many English speakers. In most parts of the world, of course, it is perfectly normal to speak two or more languages in the course of daily life. Children born in the Sylhet region of Bangladesh, for instance, speak Sylheti in the home, are taught through Bengali in school and learn Arabic in the mosque. Berber families from Algeria may switch from Kabyle to Algerian Arabic to Standard Modern Arabic to French, depending on the subject and the situation.

The children who speak English as a second (or even third or fourth) language in British schools come from many different backgrounds (Alladina & Edwards, 1991). Some have been born in the new country; others have arrived more recently, either as economic migrants or as political refugees. And there are other differences, too. For instance, some Panjabi speakers have arrived directly from rural communities in India and Pakistan; others have come from middle-class families in East Africa; they may be Muslim, Sikh or Hindu.

Some children show a strong commitment to the language of their community. They will use it with their family and friends and may spend many hours learning to read and write in special classes outside school. Others will prefer to use only English and will have perhaps only a receptive understanding of the language of their parents and their grandparents. Children learning English as a second language are by no means a homogeneous group.

To respond effectively to the needs of language learners, teachers need information in a number of key areas. For instance, which language(s) do they speak? Where do children come from? Are they familiar with another script or writing system?

Which language do they speak?

Questions about language sometimes generate very cautious replies. For instance, children may say they speak Pakistani instead of Urdu or African instead of Yoruba. The assumption — often based on hard experience — is that the person asking the question will never have heard of their language and may have little interest in finding out more.

Yet accurate information on children's language background is essential. It may be possible, for instance, to pair beginners in English with other children who speak their language and who can introduce them to class and playground routines. Teachers who create opportunities for children to speak and write their languages in the classroom, raise their status while, at the same time, broadening the knowledge of monolingual English speakers. In short, they help create an atmosphere of mutual respect.

Which country do they come from?

Children who speak the same language do not necessarily come from the same country. A Portuguese speaker can come from Portugal or Brazil. A Spanish speaker can come from Spain, Mexico or one of the many Hispanophone counties of South America. A Gujarati speaker may have come directly from India; alternatively their great-grandparents or grandparents may have settled in East Africa before political tensions forced them to move on to the UK. Many of these same families have subsequently migrated yet again to North American destinations.

Information on both the country of origin and the history of migration is important for a number of reasons. It is useful to know, for instance, that children from Sierra Leone are likely to have been educated through the medium of English, or that children from Finland start school in the year of their seventh birthday. Parents in families from rural India may have had limited access to formal education; whereas those who arrived via East Africa will have received a high level of education through the medium of English.

It is also important to be aware of the many stresses experienced by refugee children. Recent arrivals from Bosnia or Somalia, for example, may have been separated from significant family members. They may have lived in camps where they were exposed to continued violence and deprivation. Not surprisingly, children who have been traumatised in this way can be aggressive or withdrawn and need to be treated with great sensitivity.

Which religion?

Children in British schools will come from many different religious backgrounds: Chinese children may be Buddhists or followers of Confucianism, Taoism or ancestor worship. Children from the Indian sub-continent will most probably be Hindus, Muslims or Sikhs. An understanding of the main tenets of children's religion and ways in which this may impinge on their daily life, including aspects of their dress and diet, is essential.

Which writing system?

It is very important for teachers to know as much as possible about children's previous experience of literacy. There are many different possibilities (Coulmas, 1996). Very young children may have had little exposure to the written word in either English or their community language. The same will apply to children who come from poor rural settings, or whose education has been disrupted by war. In contrast, children transferring from one education system to another may be highly literate in their own language and able to use their previous experience to make rapid progress in English. Many children born in the new country will attend classes outside school to help them learn to read and write in their community language, while others have literacy skills in English only.

Teachers are better placed to help children when they have a clear picture of their prior experience. Can they read and write another language? Are they attending community language classes? Are they familiar with another script? Does this script run from left to right as in English, from right to left as in Arabic, or from top to bottom as in Japanese? Does their writing rest on an imaginary line as in English or hang from the line as in Hindi? Equally important, what is the nature of the writing system in question? Is it alphabetic as in most European languages, syllabic as in most Indian languages, a consonantal writing system as is the case in Arabic and Hebrew, or logographic as in Chinese, or Japanese *kanji*? Or is it a mixed system which draws on elements from more than one writing system as in the case of Japanese which combines two different syllabaries and logographic writing?

Promoting other Languages

In the past it was commonly believed that bilinguals could speak neither of their languages as well as monolinguals. In this view, the brain was seen as a receptacle with a fixed capacity. Today, we understand that many skills are not acquired separately: when learned in the first language, they can be transferred to second and subsequent languages (Cummins, 1996). For instance, children who learn to read in one language know that print carries meaning; that the stream of speech is broken into words, that there are conventions, such as the direction of the print; that inessential words can be skipped; that you can guess unknown words from context; and that you can read ahead when you do not know a word.

Bilingualism also has social benefits: it makes it possible to communicate within the family, particularly between generations; it gives children access to a shared history and culture; and it also opens up a wider range of careers. Bilingualism is thus seen today as an asset not a liability.

The challenge for the teacher, then, is to find ways of supporting children's bilingual development. In most cases, the main responsibility for maintaining minority languages will fall on the family and community classes. However, there are many opportunities to create an atmosphere in mainstream schooling which acknowledges and encourages children's efforts outside school.

The visual environment

The visual environment in school sends powerful messages to parents and children (Multilingual Resources for Children Project, 1995). Signs in other languages can provide information, direct and welcome visitors to the school. A wide range of commercially-made signs is now available. Alternatively, bilingual teachers and parents can help produce hand-written or word-processed signs. Other opportunities for using the languages of the school include labels and nameplates, alphabet and number charts, bilingual captions under children's drawings and bilingual notices on parent notice boards.

It is also important to look carefully at the posters and other visual materials on display. Do they reflect the children represented in the school or in the wider society? And what about the play materials? Do home corners in classrooms for younger children include cooking utensils, food packets and dressing-up clothes from other cultures? Are children exposed to a wide range of instruments in music? Can they experiment with different writing implements?

Multilingual resources

It is important to make sure that class and library resources include a range of materials in other languages, including books, newspapers, magazines, bilingual dictionaries and audiocassettes.

Bilingual stories

Dual texts — or bilingual picture books — are a regular feature of many classrooms. They can be used in a number of ways. Children can use the other language text to help them access English, or the English to help them make sense of the other language text; mixed language pairs can share the book, each reading in their own language; monolingual English speakers can speculate on what is happening in the other language; bilingual teachers can read or tell the story, first in one language then in the other; monolingual teachers can work alongside bilingual colleagues or parents.

Different writing systems

When children and parents read and write in other languages, there are many valuable opportunities for finding out about different writing systems (Edwards, 1996). Chinese children, for instance, will be able to show how they learn the different sequences of strokes that make up each distinctive character using special brushes and blocks of ink; Arabic and Urdu speakers can demonstrate how their writing goes from right to left and how the shape of the letter varies according to its position in the word, and Panjabi and Bengali speakers can show how letters hang down from the line.

Word-processing in other languages

Multilingual word-processing has enormous potential for raising the status of other languages in the classroom. It can be used for children's own writing, for making signs and labels, for communication with parents and for making books for use in the class or school library. Activities of this kind are a useful focus for developing open and trusting relations with parents.

Monolingualism _can_ be Cured

There have been enormous changes in British education in the last 30 to 40 years, both in responses and attitudes to linguistic diversity. Initially, the range of languages and cultures represented in many city classrooms was seen as a problem to be solved. Increasingly, bilingualism has come to be regarded as a resource both for individual children and for the larger school community. The knowledge and experience of parents is also being seen as a key issue in meeting the needs of bilingual children.

These optimistic statements should not, however, be taken as examples of complacency. Actual teacher awareness, knowledge and sensitivity varies enormously, and practice can sometimes be extremely patchy. There are still teachers who advise parents to speak only English at home and who have no idea of the other languages which children speak or the religions which they follow. There are still schools which have no policies on how to handle sensitive issues such as racist name-calling, or make little effort to involve parents in their children's education. Important progress has been made towards the recognition of the needs of language learners. However, much vital work remains to be done.

References

Alladina, S. and Edwards, V. (1991) *Multilingualism in the British Isles*, 2 vols. London: Longman.

Bourne, J. (1989) *Moving into the Mainstream*. Windsor: National Foundation for Educational Research.

Coulmas, F. (1996) *The Blackwell Encyclopaedia of Writing Systems*. Oxford: Blackwell.

Cummins, J. (1996) *Negotiating Identities: Education for Empowerment in a Diverse Society*. Ontario, CA: California Association for Bilingual Education.

Edwards, V. (1996) *Writing in Multilingual Classrooms*. Reading: University of Reading.

Edwards, V. and Redfern, A. (1992) *The World in a Classroom: Language and Education in Britain and Canada*. Clevedon: Multilingual Matters.

Inner London Education Authority (ILEA) (1987) *Language Census*. London: ILEA Research and Statistics.

Multilingual Resources for Children Project (1995) *Building Bridges: Multilingual Resources for Children*. Clevedon: Multilingual Matters.

Conclusions

The Educational and Linguistic Development of Japanese Children

BRIAN RICHARDS

Introduction

This volume began with a poignant reminiscence by a 13-year-old Japanese boy of his arrival in England at the age of eight. Interestingly, his account gives a preview of both the hopes and the concerns expressed by the parents, professionals and researchers who have contributed to the preceding chapters and by those we have encountered in the course of our research into Japanese families in the UK. Although the account is retrospective, the boy's note, entitled 'Leaving Japan' draws attention to his excited anticipation of leaving for a new country, and of the opportunity to learn a new language. But there are themes of loss as well: the loss of Japanese friends and the fear of losing the language of his home country. Then there is the feeling of disorientation on being surrounded by both spoken and written language which cannot be understood and the strategies used to cope: if in doubt, answer 'yes' or 'no'. Finally, in the description of school there is a sense of passive bewilderment.

It seems to me entirely appropriate that the words and feelings of a Japanese child transported into a totally new cultural, linguistic and educational environment should be used as the organising principle of this concluding chapter. The themes raised in his note will therefore be developed under the headings below.

Social-Educational Factors

There are approximately 1000 Japanese companies in the UK alone. This has resulted in a Japanese population in the country of nearly 51,000 whose length of stay will be unknown at the outset, but will probably be between three and five years (Yamada-Yamamoto, Chapter 1). We cannot, of course, take it for granted that Japanese workers and their families are willing migrants to the countries they are allocated to, although our survey (Chapter 1) did not reveal negative attitudes. However, we did obtain some sense of social isolation from mainstream British society. We found, for example, that about 70% of fathers and over 40% of mothers had very little social contact with English speakers in this country (Richards & Yamada-Yamamoto, in press).

Some sense of this isolation filters through in Yumiko Shibata's account of her son's early educational experiences in Chapter 17. Her personal testimony illustrates with a moving clarity the pressures of an enforced move for those inexperienced in living overseas. From the outset, she was deeply concerned about a lack of knowledge of the educational system in Britain and of the National Curriculum. She emphasises the importance of close contacts and good communication between Japanese parents and their children's schools. With considerable humility Mrs Shibata regrets that she is unable to deal with academic topics like some of the other contributors and claims to be merely recounting her own personal experiences as a parent. Yet her theme of relationships between parents and schools, the importance of information about the schools, the curriculum and their children's progress is one which is taken up by many of the education professionals who have contributed to this volume. In Chapter 16, for example, Mariko Sasagawa-Garmory points out how parent–teacher cooperation can support Japanese pupils and assist their adaptation to British education. Equally important, however, is that such relationships can also benefit the parent, particularly mothers who, with most fathers working long hours, bear the heaviest burden of responsibility for their children's care and education (as Sarah Mitchell informs us in Chapter 11). However, Mariko Sasagawa-Garmory sees this as a reciprocal process in which the parents also have a part to play. On the one hand, British schools need to provide information and encourage Japanese parents to question teachers and express opinions in a way which may be culturally alien to them. On the other hand, parents may have to be prepared to adjust their expectations of schools.

In the light of these concerns it is gratifying to realise that many professionals are not only in sympathy with them, but have in some cases made a practical contribution to addressing them. This can be seen, among others, in the work of the Reading Multicultural Services (Mitchell, Chapter 11), of Margaret Pond of the Mount School (Chapter 8) where special arrangements are made to involve fathers, and in the philosophy of staff at the Hillside School (Griffin & Allaway, Chapter 9) who see their reading scheme as a unifying link between child, parents, teachers and the curriculum, which involves parents closely in the development of children's literacy.

So far, I have concentrated on parents because the stresses on them are so easily forgotten in the focus on children's linguistic and educational progress. Nevertheless, the concern for children's social integration with their peers, and with their welfare and pastoral care was evident in many of the chapters in this book. This becomes clear, for example, in Julie Bunker's description of the Pre-Prep Department of Crosfields School (Chapter 10), and again in Margaret Pond's account of cultural and social activities, and special facilities for overseas pupils who occasionally need a refuge from the stresses of the classroom (Chapter 8). Viv Edwards (Chapter 21) raises the possibility of pairing new arrivals with a speaker of the same home language who would introduce them to the social and academic routines of the classroom and playground. Finally, Mo Pickering (Chapter 12) indicates that most of her colleagues who are support staff working in mainstream classrooms in Derbyshire are Japanese speaking.

Like the Japanese boy's account, however, these references are not without their tensions and conflicts. In Chapter 6, Joanna McPake comments that a belief in the uniqueness of being Japanese is, for many parents, an essential component of their cultural identity. This may be accompanied by the feeling that integration into British society means a loss of 'Japaneseness'. There are echoes of such tension between teachers' desire for social integration of Japanese pupils with their English-speaking peers and the same pupils' need to retain their national identity in Chapter 8. Here Margaret Pond shows us how this issue can bring about conflict and even bullying between Japanese pupils. This illustrates the need for teachers to be aware of such cultural issues if they are to deal with similar situations sensitively and effectively or forestall their occurrence. As indicated by the contributions of Viv Edwards (Chapter 21) and Mo Pickering (Chapter 12) the 'common-sense' view of many teachers in favour of total linguistic and cultural immersion is unlikely to be appropriate.

Educational-Cultural Issues

In Chapter 14 Emiko Furuya-Wise drew attention to the wide diversity of background of Japanese children who attend the Japanese Saturday School, and Lydia Morey reminds us in Chapter 19 of a group we often tend to forget: children sent to attend British boarding schools by parents who remain in Japan. Nevertheless, our focus here will be the same as the focus of our research: on children who are *temporarily* resident in this country. The length of stay of these children is such that, even though it is temporary, they may have difficulty in settling into Japanese schools on their return (Mitchell, Chapter 11) either because they have fallen behind linguistically and academically or because of a different educational culture. The tensions between making progress in the British educational system, and the pressure to keep up with their peers in Japan in relation to the Japanese national curriculum (Aizawa, Chapter 2; Furuya-Wise, Chapter 14) is, somewhat sadly, symbolised by the notion of 'black Friday' — the often desperate attempt to catch up with Japanese homework before attending Saturday School the following day (Aizawa, Chapter 15). But there are less obvious tensions too, and these lie in basic assumptions embedded in the school systems of each country.

In Chapter 6, Joanna McPake describes research carried out by herself and her colleague Janet Powney which has identified four main areas of dissonance experienced by Japanese pupils in British schools. A dissonance in the sense used here can be described as a clash between the educational cultures of Britain and Japan. As will be shown below, the testimony of English and Japanese professionals and Japanese parents in the chapters above have sounded frequent echoes of one of McPake and Powney's areas of dissonance in particular, thus providing further validation of their research.

Classroom talk and cultural differences in communication

The first dissonance referred to by Joanna McPake, and the one we will concentrate on here, is that the roles of talk and silence are, generally speaking, conceptualised differently. British teachers give high priority to the role of talk in learning, and speaking skills are assessed from the earliest stages of the National Curriculum. 'Talk' embraces both talk to the teacher and talk with fellow pupils. The Japanese conception is that children learn by listening to the teacher and work on their own, in silence. One finds parallels here in the cultural differences in communication and the *value* attached to talk as an activity described in my own earlier chapter (Richards, Chapter 5). Japanese conversations are frequently described as having less talk and more silence than conversations between Westerners. The communicative burden appears to be more on the *listener* than the speaker and the notion of empathy is an important one. These values appear to be embedded even in the earliest mother–child conversations. Whereas Western mothers appear to be more information oriented, interested in descriptive detail, and the exchange of information which is already known to both parties, Japanese mothers talk less and seem more concerned with caring for the child and establishing emotional bonds, and, later, with 'empathy training'.

From the perspective of a speech and language therapist, Carolyn Letts in Chapter 4 makes us aware of the possible consequences of not taking children's cultural background into account when making assessments. Cultural variation in the circumstances under which it is appropriate to talk, in body language, and the use of eye contact can easily give a completely false impression to the uninformed. This is equally true of many contexts of educational assessment, including linguistic assessment. Julie

Bunker (Chapter 10) and Sarah Mitchell (Chapter 11) confirm the reluctance of many Japanese pupils to speak much or to join in discussion and Mitchell emphasises the concerns of teachers in respect of National Curriculum assessments.

The importance attached to talk in the process of learning is seen by Mo Pickering (Chapter 12) and Viv Edwards (Chapter 21) as a powerful argument for learning through the curriculum in mainstream classrooms (with appropriate support) rather than being withdrawn and taught in special units. Pickering emphasises English as the vehicle for learning rather than a decontextualised object of study, while Edwards points out the inadequacy of the withdrawal situation to provide a sufficient range of English language experience where the teacher is the sole source of input. It is the very emphasis attached to talk and collaborative learning, she argues, as well the opportunity to have access to the whole curriculum that makes the mainstream classroom so appropriate for bilingual pupils.

Adaptations by schools

In addition to attempts to develop improved communications, and provide a better supply of information and closer links with parents, many schools also go out of their way to make cultural adaptations of their own. The chapters by Viv Edwards (Chapter 21), Ann Griffin and Sue Allaway (Chapter 9), Sarah Mitchell (Chapter 11), Mo Pickering (Chapter 12) all show ways in which schools can and do inform teachers about Japanese culture and education and cultivate sensitivity and respect for these among both teachers and pupils. In bilingual classrooms, the importance of obtaining accurate information about the languages children speak, their levels of literacy in their first language(s), and the conventions of the writing system cannot be over-emphasised.

Linguistic Issues

In recent years there has been a widening understanding of the capacity of human beings to function in multilingual contexts, a recognition that many skills are transferable between languages (Edwards, Chapter 21), and an effective assault on the myth that the development of a second language is necessarily at the expense of the first (see also Aizawa, Chapter 15). Nevertheless, several contributors to this volume (Gilhooly, Chapter 18; Ito, Chapter 20; Morey, Chapter 19; Yamada-Yamamoto, Chapter 7) signal the wide typological differences between English and Japanese, and Japanese parents have expressed many fears and concerns to us both about their children's Japanese development and what they perceive as a slow rate of development of English.

To some extent we can be reassured by the detailed case studies of Japanese children's early acquisition of English reported by Asako Yamada-Yamamoto (Chapter 7) and Michelle Turner (Chapter 13). Yamada-Yamamoto demonstrates how different areas of syntax may be mastered earlier or later by Japanese children than the expected schedule for children with English as a first language (e.g. Garman, Chapter 3) depending on their similarity to or difference from Japanese. On the other hand, many comments in this volume bear witness to the tensions that exist between the need to maintain and develop Japanese to the level of peers of the same age in Japan, and the desire to acquire a high level of competence in English. While the natural reaction of many teachers in British schools is to give English highest priority, Japanese parents and educators worry that children will not achieve a sufficient level of *academic* language and literacy in Japanese to succeed in the educational system in Japan. These concerns are expressed most strongly by Kazue Aizawa (Chapter 15) who cited cases of children who returned to Japan with 'imperfect English and imperfect Japanese'. The extent of this problem, and in what way their language can be said to be 'imperfect' in relation to the children's social, vocational and academic needs remains to be assessed and needs to be the focus of further research.

Conclusion

In Chapter 20, Kiyoko Ito describes learning a new language as 'just like finding a new world'. If this is true of English adults learning Japanese, how strange the new world must be for Japanese children learning English in the context of a different culture and through the medium of a different educational system! That so many of these children appear to flourish and achieve high levels of educational achievement is a tribute to them and their parents, but also to those teachers and educationalists who have taken account of their needs. Viv Edwards has warned us against complacency — she points out that there is considerable variation between teachers in their practice and their sensitivity to the issues discussed in this book. Mrs Shibata recounted how, in the light of her experience with her older son's education, her younger son's passage through the school system seemed relatively painless. Knowledge and experience are indispensable for parents and professionals alike, and we would regard this volume as being one means of sharing and disseminating the experience and knowledge of those who have contributed.

Reference
Richards, B.J. and Yamada-Yamamoto, A. (in press) The linguistic experience of Japanese pre-school children and their families in the UK. *Journal of Multilingual and Multicultural Development.*

Contributors

KAZUE AIZAWA The Japanese Saturday School, London
SUE ALLAWAY Hillside County Primary School, Reading
JULIE BUNKER Crosfields School, Reading
VIV EDWARDS Reading and Language Information Centre, The University of Reading
EMIKO FURUYA-WISE The Japanese Saturday School, London
MICHAEL GARMAN Department of Linguistic Science, The University of Reading
HELEN GILHOOLY Japanese Resources Centre, Derbyshire County Council
ANN GRIFFIN Hillside County Primary School, Reading
KIYOKO ITO Central Foundation Boys' School; University of Westminster, London
CAROLYN LETTS Department of Linguistic Science, The University of Reading
JOANNA MCPAKE Scottish Council for Research in Education
SARAH MITCHELL Multicultural Services, Reading
LYDIA MOREY Freelance teacher of Japanese based in Cardiff
MO PICKERING Japanese Resources Centre, Derbyshire County Council
MARGARET POND The Mount School, London
BRIAN RICHARDS School of Education, The University of Reading
MARIKO SASAGAWA-GARMORY English Cultural Centre for Japanese, London
YUMIKO SHIBATA Japanese Parent, Pinner, Middlesex
MICHELLE TURNER Department of Linguistic Science, The University of Reading
DAVID WILKINS Department of Linguistic Science, The University of Reading
ASAKO YAMADA-YAMAMOTO Department of Linguistic Science, The University of Reading

Index

spelling *see* writing
strategies 67-8

Taeschner, T. 42
Toda, S. 43

UK education *see also* reading, writing
— classroom talk 48-9, 92, 126, 136
— classroom organisation 91, 128, 130, 135
— dissonances for Japanese children 47-54, 91-2, 109-110, 114-5, 135, 136
— elitism 51
— English language support 73, 78, 88, 90, 94, 126-7
— examinations 73-5, 76, 106, 120
— higher education 51
— knowledge versus skills 49-51, 109
— mainstream classrooms 126-7, 137
— multilingual classrooms 126-31
— multilingual resources 130-131

— schools 20-1, 25, 73-89
  private, primary 87-9, 112-5
  private, secondary 73-7
  state, primary 78-86
— self assessment 83
— teacher assessment 25, 92, 137
— teacher in-service training 94
— withdrawal classes 126, 137
unanalysed utterances *see* formulae
utterance length 60-1

Wada, M. 3
Watanabe, J. 3
Wells, G. 60, 62
writing, English 78-86, 88, 89
— spelling 85, 88
— writer's workshop 78-9

Yamada-Yamamoto, A. 22, 55, 63, 67, 68, 134
Yamamoto, M. 1
Yashiro, K. 2, 3